Nicole Lusiani

nothing's missing

A Year of Reckoning, Release, and Remembering Who I Am

dirtpath
PUBLISHING

Published in the United States by Dirt Path Publishing
Contact for permissions or general inquiries - info@dirtpathpublishing.com
Contact for sales inquiries - sales@dirtpathpublishing.com

Cover Design: Toney Apalisok
Text Design: Toney Apalisok

First Edition

ISBN: 978-0-9905223-9-3
E-book ISBN: 978-0-9905223-8-6

Library of Congress Cataloging-in-Publication Data

Nicole Lusiani Elliott
Nothing's Missing: A year of reckoning, release, and remembering who I am / edited by Dirt Path Publishing -- 1st ed.
ISBN 978-0-9905223-9-3   1. Memoir   2. Self-Help

Praise For *Nothing's Missing*

From the very first sentence of *Nothing's Missing* I felt seen, heard, loved and unconditionally accepted for my messy humanity. There are very few other humans who've been able to reach out from the page to make me feel that way, and for that, I am forever in Nicole's debt. And, as someone who has been "shoulding" all over myself my entire life, what a gift that, through *Nothing's Missing*, Nicole made me feel less alone AND helped me to see that there's another way. "Fine sucks," indeed. *-Michele Rehinhart, Educator, Mother*

A story of reckoning with the tension of romantic love, betrayal, and self love in the face of fear and grace. Through observing her own vulnerability, Nicole will reveal vulnerability to the reader, themselves. *-Dr. Carrie Wasson, Psychologist, Mother*

Nicole's story inspires readers to take the time to honor their authentic selves without the pressure of the many roles we hold in life. She reminds us to always search for our peace, whatever it may look like, no matter how hard the journey. *-Lauren Midgette, Educator, Mother*

As someone who is also a recovering perfectionist, Nicole's powerful memoir really knocked me over when she articulated this statement, "In short, *Should* is a real asshole." In releasing herself from the power of *Should*, she also released something in me. What would it mean to be free from *Should* and, instead, focus on the potential of now? That may just be what freedom is. *-Tessa Yeager, Educator*

I read this book in one sitting and cannot wait to read it again. Next time, I want to tag pages and highlight phrases - there are so many that both inspired and challenged me. The emotions and insights were raw and real - moving me to draw analogies to my own life and goals in ways that I didn't expect. *-Linda, Project Management, Mother, Grandmother*

Nicole's beautiful writing addresses the darkness of struggle through a fresh, honest, memoir. We learn from her, witnessing how a life can be lifted through the alchemy of courage, faith, and self-care. I was inspired by her story. *-Martha Van Buskirk, Writer, Mother*

Nicole captures the essence of what is true for so many people - in our quest to live our lives the way we think we should, we lose sight of who we are and what is important. In her journey to move forward in a more meaningful way, we gain insight about how to rethink what is important in life. I've gained a whole new appreciation for wildflowers - and so many other things that don't grow in rows. *-Traci Everett, Educator, Mother, Grandmother*

Nicole shares her own journey and her ultimate trust in embracing what life has to offer so beautifully in this debut memoir. As a 50 year-old woman with many of the same fears and expectations, I really leaned into both her struggle and, ultimately, how her grace was revealed. Thanks to this lovely read, I will never take that dog walk for granted; instead, I will see it as a way to find my quiet and see my truth. *-Erin Rogge, HR Compliance Industry, Mother*

Nothing's Missing is an honest and vulnerable story of a woman who lost herself somewhere between childhood and the pursuit of the American Dream. Nicole dares to ask, "Is the life I thought I should have the one I really want?" and, in doing so, she gives the reader courage to ask herself the same question. The answer has the power to set us all free. *Nothing's Missing* isn't about do ing what's right; it's about doing, and being, what's true. -*Angie Mizzell, Mother, Lifestyle blogger, Author of* Girl in the Spotlight

Nicole's warmth of spirit and depth of humanity radiate from each sentence, reaching toward her reader like a bold wildflower, calling us to live more completely, fully, and peacefully. With boundless courage, relentless honesty, and a bit of wry humor, Nicole unwraps her story and the lessons she has learned from it in this memoir. While the details of Nicole's story are her own, the lessons she so clearly and wisely shares are for each of us who are striving onward in our noisy, busy lives, perhaps suspecting that a more complete life is possible. Nicole's words point us to the missing pieces we already hold within. Read this book if you have been through a journey, if you seek a kindred spirit, if you have somehow lost touch with yourself along your pursuit of happiness. Read this book if you are doing a hard thing and need inspiration, if you long for an authentic conversation with a friend, if you've ever received the wholehearted love of a dog or an Italian grandma, or if ocean smells and wildflowers stir your heart. -*Kathryn McRi*tche, *Educator, Mother*

Soulful, insightful, inspiring! Nicole loves her people hard and her words always make me feel a little braver. -*Tricia Cramer, Semiconductor Industry, Mother*

Nicole's undauntedness in pursuit of her peace and her individual truth commenced a much needed exhale for me, along with permission to feel all the things that have been stuffed down and bottled up. I'm grateful. -*Lydia McClanaha*n, *Educator, Mother*

Nothing's Missing shows us all how life demands re-examination of our experiences and expectations to chart our paths forward. A must read! -*Pamela Wilson, Educator, Mother, Grandmother*

A mirror tells all, the details you love and the flaws you don't. In this incredible testimony to self love above all, Nicole brings the reader to that mirror, allowing us the closest of looks so that we, too, may find love less elusive and wholly present. *Nothing's Missing* is a true gift of self, a vulnerable story of strength, courage and love. *-Carrie Eicher, Educator, Mother*

So many of the themes that run through this story are relatable to my own heart and mind. Not only am I also a people pleaser with good hair, I have lived my life struggling with anxiety, depression, and dammit, have passed these along to 2 of 3 of my children. Nicole has the undeniable talent of being able to put into words what many of us face but struggle to articulate. *-Kimberly McGowen, Interior Designer, Mother*

Laced with up-close vulnerability and wisdom.
-Tovi C. Scruggs-Hussein, Educator, Speaker, Author

Honest and vulnerable, poetic and funny.
-Nora Clark, Educator, Mother

Nothing's Missing is a beautiful story written with a vulnerability that is both unique and important in a world where people are socialized to keep their guard up. Since reading it I have found myself leaning into greater honesty and vulnerability with others about my ideas and feelings with greater confidence. *-Nancy Ogden, Educator, Mother*

As we age and life changes, the world can seem a bit lonelier at times. This book reminds us we are not alone; in fact, we are one, experiencing similar paths as we navigate our individual lives. This will be one of those books that I pick up and read again, here and there, from time to time, for comfort as I continue to walk through my own journey. *-Denise Stracner, Registered Nurse, Mother*

Nicole has crafted a piece of art that cannot be passed by. She missed nothing when it comes to life – all the crazy, happy, sad, and joyous times we sometimes overlook. She reminded me that in the hardest times of life, stopping to just love on your dog can bring me back to square one. If you are feeling like something is missing, pick up this book and you, too, will realize, maybe the thing that was missing from your life was you. - *Alissa Pacheco, Dental Hygienist, Mother*

For Thomas Antonio and Jackson Giovanni,
who belong among the wildflowers.

And for you, who deserves to feel free.

CONTENT

INTRODUCTION

Dear Friend,

Every few years I come to some really hard conclusions about what it takes to shake off the *shoulds* and embrace the truth of who I *am*. I have these incredible breakthroughs and, then, life goes on. Somewhere between packing lunches and walking dogs and arguing about the grocery list, a full-time job, raising kids, caring for elders…I get lost again. A few years go by and, even though I'm more myself than I was before, I find myself again doing the dance of should to prove to everybody—to myself—that everything is *fine*.

The clarity from any earlier breakthroughs fades and I begin to unconsciously aspire, once again, to nothing more than fine. Don't make waves. *You're fine, just be cool.* Next thing I know I'm back – for reasons I still don't understand - in resistance to everything that brings me joy and power and light.

The truth? *Should* is a real jackass. And fine sucks.

Several years ago, I hit the place where the pain of a given situation outweighed the pain of making a change: my carefully constructed identity was cracking, my marriage was falling apart, and my struggle with anxiety could no longer be contained. Only when we rescued a dog that had a boundless energy, requiring several miles a day of walking, did I find the courage to face these truths.

We'd walk morning, noon, and night on a dirt path near my house that ran by the water. On this path are huge bunches of yellow wildflowers. Long and lanky, reaching tall toward the sun, simple and beautiful and completely un-manicured. They were fully themselves, in all of their perfect imperfection. They were the opposite of "fine." They were free.

Early one morning Mario and I walked by them and I thought, Those wildflowers right there, they are everything I want to be.

Wildflowers don't grow in rows, I thought, as we passed them again on our way home, *and neither do I*.

I decided at that very moment to stop pretending. To stop hiding in the name of trying to be perfect. To release the idea that everybody else has it all together and therefore I should, too. This book captures the essence of that year-long journey to reckon with what I had allowed my life to become, learn how to release the shoulds, and remember who I am: not "fine," but simple, beautiful, imperfect, and free.

I came through that experience wanting to stop living a constructed life and start thriving under my own unique set of circumstances in exactly the way God created me to. I want to stand tall in my light, making it bright enough for others to see their own. I want you and me and all of us to light up the world with our gifts.

Wildflowers don't grow in rows, and neither do I.

Wildflowers don't grow in rows, and neither do you.

There is liberation in saying, my house is a mess, my children are sometimes ill-mannered, I am insecure some days and need reassurance most days. There is liberation in knowing I'm tired of *fine* and I'm tired of *should*, and I'm ultimately tired of the bullshit that is tied up with trying to live life so carefully that I never disappoint anyone, only to end up chronically disappointing myself.

Ultimately what brought me to this courage, in addition to the unconditional devotion of my dog, was my desire to liberate myself in service to liberating my children. Children "evangelize" us, I was told once by a priest who was baptizing my oldest son, whether we're ready or not. I'm not sure he meant it this way, but freeing myself to free them, even if it scares the shit out of me, is exactly how I'm living his lesson.

I didn't want to write this book; it's personal and painful and doing so leaves me feeling deeply exposed. It tells the often unspoken story of what happens after a spouse has been unfaithful but the couple decides to stay together anyway. Interestingly enough, it's not at all a story about marriage. It's a story of me reckoning with the fact that, above all else, I was actually the one who was unfaithful. Over and over again, I was unfaithful to myself.

I wrote this book for me, so I'd never again forget who I am. Every time I walked by the manuscript that I had shelved more than a decade before, I felt my heart pull toward it. This story, it wouldn't leave me alone. The global pandemic and the struggle that came with it sparked a deeper fire–that fire of outrageous courage that is as terrifying as it is compelling. That fire told me I'd forgotten the lessons from the years before and I had begun to betray myself once again. I looked around at the women I love and saw them doing the same. The unceasing voices in our heads com-

16

paring our suffering, shaming ourselves, telling us how we should be grateful because we're *fine*.

We've all been given a piece to life's puzzle and we're not going to get anywhere individually or collectively until we're each able to unabashedly put that piece down on the table with everyone else's. Each of us with our unique gifts, perfectly designed just as they should be, not contorted into some socially acceptable standard of what someone else thinks it should be. If we are going to change the world into a place where we want our children to grow old, then we have to allow ourselves the Grace of stepping into the lives we were created to live, not the lives other people think we *should*.

Grace is calling us. I know it. Just as I know most of us have something that is muffling that call. I'd be willing to bet what's causing the muffle for each of us is an old coping mechanism or patterned way of being that has lost its utility in this, our grown up life. I struggle with anxiety that has roots in childhood pain and brain chemistry but is perpetuated by the fact that I continue to abandon vibrancy in exchange for *fine*. I can't change the first two, but I sure as hell can change the last.

So can you. And we must. God created us to move into the fullness of our lives. We can't do everything, but, as Mother Teresa says, we can all do small things with great love. Love requires courage. Outrageous courage. A rage of fire that propels us toward that courage. Toward one another. Toward love.

That fire in me? It's in you, too. We are being called to use it to reach forward, back, and sideways, circling our wagons in favor of the truth. The truth that we are all connected. The truth that we belong to one another. The truth that we've come way too far to tolerate *fine*.

When I think of the women who made my life possible, I am humbled. I'm also a little ashamed. My grandmothers and their mothers and my mother, they all sacrificed so much so that I could live the life I have right now. In many cases, my *fine* would be their dream. But I also know they didn't create me just to stop there. They created me so I would move forward and bring others with me.

The world is out of balance for many reasons, one being because women have been trained to play small for far too long. Those before us fought valiantly so we wouldn't have to do that anymore. They knew that, when we reach tall toward the sun, the possibilities are endless, and, as that revolution occurs, the world turns upside right again.

This is my call to action. To reach tall toward the sun, where we live into the unique gifts we've been given along with everyone else and the possibilities for our individual and collective well-being are endless. My intention in writing this very personal story that is difficult for me to share is that you, too, might hear your call.

I wrote this book from my vantage point, from my memory, and with all the biases that come from only one side of the story. I may have made some mistakes along the way, misinterpreted, mis-remembered. That said, I did my best to honor the people involved and tell as true of a story as I could. I had my husband, Craig, read it, and offered him the chance to let me know what he wanted to be left out, even offering to put the book to bed right there and then, if it was something that was too difficult for him to be made public. "It's your story, Nicole. Not mine." he said. "Go out there and tell that story."

This, my friends, among many other reasons, is why I love this man as I do.

One final note before we begin: the dog doesn't die in the end, so you don't need to read the last chapter first to brace yourself for it. He lays at my feet as I type this, now a pile of old bones that limps from one spot to another, wearing pants so he doesn't dribble pee everywhere he goes. I will lose him soon, but not yet. He still loves a walk more than his own life. He still loves to roll on his back in the grass and make joyful honking noises. He still helps me see things that I sometimes take for granted and remember things I didn't know I'd forgotten. He still loves me, more today, it seems, than ever. Ultimately, the space he holds in my heart for what he was and what he continues to be is what gave me the strength to share this book with you, finally, after all these years.

Dog. God Backwards. No coincidence.

PROLOGUE

For months I've been asking God to help me find some quiet. My mind is so busy, my days are so full, I teach 180 students and, while I work among the best in the business, I also work in a system that doesn't value me, or my time, or my well-being. Then I come home to my own kids who are so small and need so much... where, God, can I find just a moment of quiet just for me?

Then we got our dog. And for 30 minutes, twice a day, I had quiet.

Funny thing about quiet. As soon as it comes, the truth comes with it. Quiet is the all-call for any demon, any fear, any anything from which we hide. There's no way around because they block the way forward and the way back. The only way through them is to be brave enough to hear what they have to say, allowing the fire of outrageous courage first to warm us, then to fuel us for the journey of reckoning ahead.

No wonder I've kept myself so busy for so long; if I'm busy, then I don't have to deal with the truth. If I allow myself to be still, however, if I allow myself to be quiet, then I allow myself to hear. Enter quiet, enter truth.

Damn that quiet.

Hear the Call

"It is the peculiar nature of the world
to go on spinning no matter what kind
of heartbreak is happening."

- Sue Monk Kidd, *The Secret Lives of Bees*

We'd been looking for a dog for months (or, I should say, Jackson and I have been looking for a dog, and Tommy and Craig are merely putting up with us). As we'd done several times, Jackson and I went online, and, this time, found a dog that fit our profile of a "good dog" at the Oakland Animal Shelter. Tom was at preschool and Craig was at work, so we looked at each other and simultaneously said, "Let's go!"

As we pulled up to the shelter, Jackson was so excited that he started taking his seat belt off before I had even stopped the car. Through the doors of the entrance before I took my keys out of the ignition, he was talking to a woman at the front desk by the time I caught up to him. "I'm sorry, young man," the animal control officer said, "All of the volunteers are busy right now. No one is here to bring you back to see the dog you're looking for."

Crestfallen, Jackson's shoulders drooped. For his disappointment and my own, mine did as well.

"I'm going on a break," she noted with a marked change in her tone, "maybe I can take you back on my way." I'd wager she'd never seen two pairs of identical blue eyes light up so fast.

Officer Sharon took us back and, on the way to find the dog we came to meet, we passed almost 200 dogs waiting for someone to love them as they spent their days in individual cells, not unlike a prison. As we passed through those barred corridors, we expressed potential interest in many dogs and, each time, she told us why it wasn't a good choice for a family. We paused for one she suggested we check out, but we had only two disqualifiers (male, pit bull) and he was both of them.

I knew the reputation of American Pitbulls was, at best, over-generalized and, at worst, a literal death sentence depending on the state they lived in, but I couldn't shake the *should*, or in this case, the *shouldn't*. I have two young children. I shouldn't take any chances. As to the gender disqualifier, exactly how many boys is enough for one girl to live with?

Finally, we got to the dog we came to see and, after some time in the visiting room with her, we decided we liked her a lot. She was sweet and beautiful, albeit a little younger than we wanted and very "puppy" as she circled the room, stopping only to chew on the side of the chair. Jackson gave me the huge, "Please, Mommy, I love her" eyes and, just before I said yes, the dog that Officer Sharon suggested came to mind.

I watched her watching my son with this puppy. Officer Sharon was not an animal loving volunteer whose job was to uncondi-tionally love the dogs kept at the shelter. She was an animal control officer, a member of the police department, someone the pub-lic calls on to catch strays that seem too dangerous to approach, someone who cleans up roadkill. Officer Sharon wasn't looking to match a puppy with a little boy, she was looking to find a home for a very special dog who continued to get overlooked. She was doing so not because she thought we would love him, but because she loved him.

"Officer," I started, "tell me again about that dog you suggest-ed." A volunteer had arrived back from his break and offered to go get him for us. "No," Officer Sharon said, this time with her eyes sparkling, "I'll go get Magic."

Jackson's eyebrows raised as he looked at me and mouthed, "Magic?"

The volunteer took the puppy out and Officer Sharon brought Magic in. Dark brown with a big white spot on his chest, he was so malnourished we could see his ribs. He had been pulled out of an overgrown front yard filled with stolen shopping carts about three months prior. Officer Sharon thought he was intended to be a guard dog of some kind because the neighbors had called in complaining about his barking at all hours of the day and night.

"Maybe he was supposed to be a guard dog," she said, "but, beyond the barking, he failed miserably at the task."

Officer Sharon continued, "I approached the yard and he came to me immediately," she said. "He melted into me, a love from the moment I met him." She informed the volunteers that they were to take care of him, find him a good home and, until he got that home, she would be the one to care for his nasty eye infection after each of her shifts, even when those shifts ended in a neighborhood far from the shelter. He had been here for months, she said, and his eyes had long cleared. But still, to her surprise, he hadn't found a family.

As if waiting for his introduction to come to a close, Officer Sharon looked down at Magic and only then did he walk in. He sat down at our feet, looked up at us with the brown eyes only an old soul could have, and put his chin on Jackson's knee. Anyone (or anything) that loves my child with immediate and unwavering devotion will have my immediate and unwavering loyalty forever.

Bye-bye pretty puppy, hello malnourished pit bull.

This would be the first of many shoulds I'd be releasing that year.

Officer Sharon walked him through the cat area per our request. With two cats already at home, this was his mile to walk, a chance to win a real home or lose one. On the way he passed several bunny cages and, while curious, nothing came of it. In the cat area he went up to the cage and sniffed a kitten; she arched her back at him, and he backed off.

Shelter policy dictates that all people living in the home had to be present at the adoption, so we went home to gather the skeptics. After a long family meeting, Tommy remained the holdout. At three years old and about three feet tall, he wasn't sure a big dog was a good decision. Also tired of being the smallest, and the youngest, this was a child who needed some power and, as intuitive as he has always been, he knew this was the time to take it.

"He sounds big," Tommy said. "I don't like big dogs. I don't want him. You can't make me want him."

"What if I let you name him?" Jackson asked. The glint in Tommy's eye told me he knew this was a moment to savor.

"Okay," he relented, after a deftly staged dramatic pause, "I'll take your deal. His name will be Mario." Cars was the movie of choice in those days and he remembered our delight when one of the cars in the movie was named Mario, after the famous driver, Mario Andretti. Quickly he added one more clause to the unwritten contract, looking at me with dark brown eyes and furrowed brow, "But Jackson has to promise Mario won't jump on me." My own eyebrows raised, and I looked at Jackson, who could not promise fast enough.

The next morning, we were at the shelter when it opened to pick up Mario, as excited as we were nervous. Apparently, Mario felt the same as he initially refused to get in the car. When we got home, however, he walked in like this was the place he had called home his whole life. Then, we discovered what I consider some kind of miracle: he was already housebroken. I hadn't thought to ask Officer Sharon this. Come to think of it, I hadn't thought to ask her anything.

When I got up to walk Mario the next morning, he was so grateful to see me, I think if he were human he would've cried. We took a long walk (more exercise than I've had in three years) and we came home feeling like we must be the luckiest two living creatures on earth.

I had been feeling a deep and unnamed longing for months, years even. Maybe Mario was what I had been missing in my home and my heart, this dog in dire need of rescuing by a woman in dire need of the same.

When Mario came to us, long walks every morning and evening became something else I didn't know I needed: time to think. The time I spent walking out by the water and back through the neighborhoods were initially filled with thoughts about my kids, the house, work, sometimes my husband; never, however, were those hours out in the peace and quiet been a time for me to think about me.

I think lots of parents don't consider themselves. Or maybe they do and it's just me who doesn't. I know that Craig does. He sees something he wants and goes after it while I see something I want and spend an eternity figuring out if I can make it happen, how it will impact my family, whether or not it's too much to ask. By the time I get done thinking, it's either too late or I've talked myself out of it. I feel like he makes decisions in isolation and I resent him for it. Maybe he does consider us but just doesn't communicate it? What I do know is my head is one noisy place. Even if someone asked what I wanted to do or be or have, I don't think I'd know how to answer.

When Jackson was born, the work to break him free of my body created such an enormous strain that, since then, I often feel like an old woman. Exhausted further by meeting the needs of a sensitive baby with a painful tummy, during the six years he's been alive, my heart has never been fuller, but my body also feels like it has never been less my own.

In these six years, I've devoted most of who I am and what I do to him and Tommy, his brother three years his junior, equally sensitive and equally sweet. What could be more deserving of my life's focus than honoring these two human blessings by being the best mother I could be?

Trouble is, while I thrive as a parent, I often retreat as a partner. Craig does the same. We struggle daily with communication. He continues to do things for himself when I feel like I can't. The tension in the air is palpable and everything just feels so damned hard.

A few years ago, Craig made a choice that dealt what felt like a fatal blow to our marriage. He came to me with the truth of his infidelity and, because he did, I eventually agreed to his request that we work to untangle our marital issues and try again. While he made the decision to seek respite outside our marriage, I really did know we both contributed to the mess that got us there so it felt like the right thing to own my part and give it another try. It's pretty clear now that I didn't do the work I needed to do before making that decision because I remember thinking, "Damn, I'm amazing for being able to overcome betrayal and move forward," not something someone who is really ready to own her part and do the work says to herself.

Now I'm left with the "achievement" of "saving" my marriage, and where has it gotten me? Through the hurt, maybe, but stuck in resentment.

I've read that the Buddha says this about resentment: "It's like drinking poison and expecting the other person to die." Craig is certainly not dying, but sometimes I feel like I am.

So now, thanks to Mario, I walk a lot. We walk the bay trail every day, twice a day, and I pray for the quiet I need to spark an internal reconnection with myself, so long ago lost in the love I have for my family and the fear I have in repeating mistakes that were made before me.

When I was in the fourth grade, our class had a reading contest. The student who read the most pages over winter vacation would get a new box of school supplies the first day back. If there was one thing I liked more than reading, it was school supplies. I'm not at all what someone would call "competitive," but in this case? Nothing was going to stand between me and winning.

I had two teachers in the fourth grade; it was an experiment with two classes sharing one large space, allowing kids to flow back and forth between lessons at their own pace, providing rich learning opportunities for them in the process. My teachers were Susan and Bob, two people who had a 1970s vibe in most ways, including their dislike of the false sense of authority established by adults through the titles of Mr. and Mrs.

After announcing the contest and describing the coveted prize, Susan stepped back to reveal the shelves of books from which to choose. Because we were a combination class there were sixty of us; easily one hundred books lay before us. While the readers scrambled to be first to pick the longest books, and the kids less interested in reading hustled for the shorter books, I sat back and let them all choose. One by one the students went up to choose their book. As they did, Susan gave each student a book bag, a canvas one with a happy face on it and a slogan something like, "I love to read!" I lay in wait.

"Nicole, come on up and get your book," Bob called.

"I'd rather wait until after school, if that's okay," I replied. "That way I can take my time to choose from what is left."

"Whatever works for you," replied Bob, falling easily into the laid back way of being that allowed the little people their own autonomy.

As the day wound down and the bell signaled for everyone to leave, I got my lunch box and my sweater and headed up toward the books.

"Susan," I said quietly. I was a social girl, maybe even a little flirty for a nine-year-old, but painfully earnest when it came to serious matters. And to me, most things were serious matters.

"Yes, Nicole? Are you ready to pick your book?"

"Well, yes. But I wonder about something. If the goal is to read the most pages, would it be okay if I took more than one book?" She raised her eyebrows as if to say, "Well you little devil..."

Instead she said, "Of course." With that, I took every book I could fit into my new book bag. That smiley face was bursting at the seams.

In addition to being rather serious for a typical nine-year-old, I was also very thin. I was average height but my legs took up over two thirds of my body and, as if that wasn't enough, my limbs were like sticks—"Bird Legs" I think I was called on more than one occasion. To make matters worse, my mom always liked me to wear dresses to school (with matching bows, of course). So there I was in December, two bird legs sticking out from under a dark green dress, green ribbons braided into my hair, with my stick arms lugging a lunch box, a sweater, and a bag stuffed with books.

I got to the corner of where I needed to cross the street to meet my babysitter feeling like my arm might fall off—the kind of sensation you get when you are about to lose feeling but not quite, so it hurts like hell. The crossing guard looked somewhere between amused and concerned.

"That's quite a heavy load for a little lady like yourself," he said, holding up the stop sign with one hand, calling me forth with his other, whistle half hanging out of his mouth and crinkly blue eyes smiling at me.

"Yeah, I have some work to do over vacation," I replied.

"Well, good luck with all that; but let someone help you with all those books for goodness sake. That's too much burden for one little girl to carry."

"Okay," I said, with zero intention of keeping my word. I may have had stick arms and bird legs and crazy ribbon hair, but I was strong, and no one was going to think I couldn't handle carrying all those books. When I got home, I released my arms' burden onto my bed in a bit of a huff. Would the crossing guard have said those things to a boy, I asked myself? I thought not.

I stayed in that bed with my books for three days, emerging only for the bathroom and a little food, every time returning quickly to my stacks. On the third day, I was done. I returned to school that January, triumphant. I had, indeed, read the most pages. And that school supply box was all mine.

***

That memory has stayed with me all these years for a number of reasons: Bob and Susan's respect for my peers and me, how they turned reading into something to be met with gusto, the box that now holds school supplies for my students when they win little contests in my classes, and the kindly old gentleman who took interest in my heavy load, advising me to get help and wishing me well on my journey.

And what a journey it has been. Not until this year did I realize that his advice to lighten my load is now thirty-six years in the making. Thirty-six years of me carrying way more than was ever necessary. Thirty-six years I've armed myself with accomplishments, achievements, order and control—all in the name of what?

In my life's smiley-faced book bag are countless items I carry with me, most of them based on fear. It's not just the fear of not being special, it's also even more irrational and heart wrenching fears. They go on and on, these imagined tragedies, followed closely by my plans for survival, all attempts to prepare me for anything that could possibly happen. This is how some people struggle with anxiety: we spin and spin until we collapse under the weight of the stories we tell ourselves. We are exhausted, but we can't let anyone know. We put a smile on our faces as big as the smile on that book bag while our minds race and our backs break.

We want to let it all go but we fear that, if we do, we will be unprepared for what awaits us. It's killing us, but we have to do it.

Don't we?

That's what I thought. All these years and all these accomplishments and all these plans for survival, and where am I? I'm in a lovely home with a respectable career and two gorgeous children, but I'm also in an emotional distress I wouldn't wish on anyone.

I'm so tired of fighting myself. My heart hurts. My body hurts. My mind is exhausted. I have to lay down some of my load, open my arms wide, and embrace the faith I say I have. I have to stop planning for trouble. I have to stop achieving at the sake of my own health. I have to trust the people I love and myself. I have to let go and surrender to whatever will be.

I'm afraid. I'm afraid of a thousand things. But I refuse to internalize those fears anymore. When I am hurting, I have to share it. When I need help, I have to ask for it. I'm going to release what I can and then look the other things straight in the eye.

I won't be afraid of you anymore.

This is a big step for me, and one I don't take lightly. One about which I'm sure I'll falter. But, I have to remember that, even as strong as I am, I'm not strong enough to carry the weight of the world.

I have to put my book bag down.

I think anything worth doing is worth doing well; I also think anything worth doing is likely going to be a challenge, especially when it comes to unraveling the wounds of the heart. Something about moving two steps forward, one step back, two steps forward, one step back—it keeps you clear about where you're going and where you've been. It inevitably creates a bit of a test, positing the question, *Just how serious are you about your healing?* This frustrates me, but I think it may also be necessary. Two steps forward, one step back; two forward, one back; until one day, those two steps forward bring you exactly where you need to be: ready to face the lesson you've been spending all this time trying to avoid.

This heart mending is the work of the soul and my theory is that a lesson can only be learned when you're back at where it began, facing whatever or whomever brought you that lesson into your life, with a depth of understanding you cultivated along the way. If we engage the lesson consciously with clarity, wisdom, and courage, this circular path is short. The longer we avoid that lesson, however, by pretending or numbing or any of the other things we do when we are afraid, the longer and more treacherous the path extends. I know, at least for me, that my soul sits at the center of several circles, all correlating to the series of lessons I came to this earth to learn but have, heretofore, been trying to avoid.

The circle I'm walking now feels like it will never end. I don't even know what this lesson is yet, but I'm sure it's related to a pervasive restlessness and an unthinkable resistance to anything that's good for me. Every time I get close to understanding, something in me panics and I distract myself with a new project, a new hobby, a new something that gives me focus and direction, slowing the spin of my mind and quieting the engine in my nervous system so I can breathe again.

The thing is, it never ends up being enough. I inevitably stumble back into a void of restlessness that sends me searching again, resisting the real lesson I need to learn in favor of searching for what's missing. It kind of reminds me of the children's book, *The Missing Piece*, by Shel Silverstein. What is it? What's missing? A baby? A dog? A different job?

This morning I pulled on my shoes, nudged Mario out of his bed, and opened the door to the cool, foggy morning air you only find when you live near the coastline. I walked along the bay to the waking sounds of gulls and herons, the jingle-jangle of Mario's collar, and the thump-thumping of my own feet.

There was something meditative about this walk, a cacophony that somehow came together and created a rhythm.

"Jingle-jangle-jingle."

"Thump-thump-thump."

"Jingle-jangle-jingle."

"Thump-thump-thump."

Nothing's missing.

I stopped and so did Mario. *Who is that talking? Is that me?* I stopped to look around. I saw nothing, heard nothing. Shaking my head slightly, we continued down the path.

"Jingle-jangle-jingle."

"Thump-thump-thump."

Nothing's missing. I heard it that time more clearly.

"Jingle-jangle-jingle."

"Thump-thump-thump."

Nothing's missing. That's the lesson you are refusing to learn.

Nothing's Missing. I kept trying to grapple with what this meant but, every time I started to get somewhere, something interfered: one of my boys needed a band aid, the other needed help tying his shoes, the dog chewed up the screwdriver, my husband needed his dissertation edited... I kept allowing all these things to get in my way.

Most mothers do that, right, put everything else before themselves? There is honor in that, isn't there? Or are we actually choosing to live unconsciously because it's easier than confronting what's wrong? I think my unconsciousness these past few years has been a form of emotional survival, or maybe denial. Likely both. Whatever it was, I know it served as a way for me not to have to face what I've allowed myself to become: a weary, resentful, shadow of my former self.

To shake off the blues I sometimes take my kids to the beach because I need the fresh air and they love to dig in the sand for what seems like forever. It feels futile to me, this digging, until their shovel hits some resistance and they delight in the fact they finally got deep enough to find wet sand. With wet sand, they can build a castle.

While watching them do this digging on a recent trip to the coast I was reminded of a time when I was little and went to the beach with my babysitter. Unlike the other kids, I felt overwhelmed by castle building. Isn't this hole good enough? It's a pretty cool thing to have a hole; you can sink your feet into it and cool off; you can grab handfuls of it and throw it at your friends and laugh together until your stomach hurts. *The hole is good enough,* I thought to myself.

But it wasn't, and I knew it. I sat in this hole for a really long time and then something in me shifted and I actually wanted to build. I learned finding the balance between wet and dry sand was critical, or else my castle wouldn't stand. And even when it did, I knew a wave or some mean kid was right around the corner waiting to smash all my work. Yet I built, because something in me told me it was time.

"What are you building?" my babysitter asked.

"I'm not sure yet," I answered. But I smiled because I knew, whatever it was, it was going to be great.

Fear rose again. It was hard work. I was tired. But the voice kept saying, *Build.*

I hesitated. Then started. Then hesitated. Then started.

Keep going.

And I did.

Nicole Lusiani

Set Your Intention

"Ask for what you want.
And then be prepared to get it."

- Dr. Maya Angelou

Colonoscopy. There's a word you don't associate with anything joyful. Yet, today, I sat in the doctor's office waiting for a nurse to call my name and I felt an overwhelming sense of joy.

Let's not be mistaken; preparing for this colonoscopy was traumatic. Emotionally and physically exhausted as a result, my husband dropped me off on his way to work with a kiss on the cheek and a look of worry in his eyes.

"Are you going to be okay?" he asked. "Do you want me to cancel my meeting and stay?"

No, I didn't. I don't like suffering in public, and having a camera shoved where the sun don't shine is something I was not about to share, even with the man who'd seen me through childbirth, twice. Once to a child with a head so big the doctor said, "Wait, measure that again, that can't be right," (it was) and another to a child that tipped the scales at almost ten pounds.

Nope, not sharing the colonoscopy, even with him.

"I'm okay, just really tired."

I really was just so tired. The trauma of prepping for this procedure brought me to the place of what my mom used to call "bone tired." The kind of tired that made me feel I just couldn't take one more step.

And yet I did. I always do.

After checking in I sunk into a chair in the waiting room and pulled out *Eat, Pray, Love*, a book I've been waiting to read for quite a while. As a teacher and a mother, it's not often I get to read for pleasure anymore. Something about this book, however, was calling me; I had to find a way to read it, even if that meant doing so in a doctor's office waiting for a colonoscopy, not sure if I could keep my eyes open past page two.

Turns out, I could keep my eyes open; in fact, I almost couldn't blink, especially when I got to a passage that talked about being lost in the woods. You're lost but you don't realize it because you're thinking you've just wandered off the path a bit and, soon, you'll be back on track. That's how I've felt for the last several years.

It continued,

Then night falls again and again and you still have no idea where you are and it's time to admit that you have bewildered yourself so far off the path that you don't even know from which direction the sun rises anymore.

There I was. In those pages. I almost couldn't avert my eyes for fear that if I did, I might lose myself again. How did I get here, to this doctor's office, to this way of being? I just kept thinking I had wandered off the path a few feet when, in reality, I didn't even know from which direction the sun rose any more.

I am 36 years old getting a colonoscopy because no one can figure out the cause of the pain in my pelvis. "You have colon cancer in your family history, so let's check to be sure," my doctor says. Between the fact that I may have colon cancer and I've just realized I don't know from which direction the sun rises any more, you'd think I'd be distraught.

Not so, however. Not so because, in reading this book, I've seen myself. Elizabeth Gilbert is giving me a new kind of hope, one that not only assures me that I'm not crazy, but that I just might find my way through it. I can't go to Italy and India and Indonesia; but I can go inside my own heart just as she did, and maybe, just maybe, I might find some answers. The answers that have eluded me for years may actually have been with me the whole time.

Nothing's Missing. That's the lesson you are refusing to learn.

There, in a doctor's office waiting for a colonoscopy, I was giddy with possibility.

Sometimes I dream that I'm diving into clear blue water, which is funny because I never learned to dive. Easily twenty people tried to teach me, but I could never get beyond a face plant. The fact is, this has also happened with riding a bike, singing, water skiing and just about any other thing I tried and could never quite get my body to accomplish.

In this dream, however, the dive is flawless and the water is warm and I can see all around me with perfect clarity. I get toward the bottom of the ocean floor and my uninhibited clarity and sense of security cracks. I become afraid. I quickly turn up toward the water's surface and gasp for air. Then I wake up.

It's profound, this dream, and it stays with me most of the day when I have it the night before. On those days I can often tap into a real (albeit fleeting) recognition of my issues around perfectionism and control. And then it's gone, almost like, if I allow myself to graze the bottom of that ocean floor, I might die. I panic and swiftly stride toward the familiar, ascending to the surface powered by the adrenaline of a child being chased by a big, barking dog.

This dream makes me wonder, *Is this anxiety, the anxiety I'm just starting to realize has been with me my whole life, a tool for avoiding what's really bothering me? A habituation of sorts, that I've designed to protect me from my real fear?*

I know I was an exceptionally sensitive child, but it's just recently that I am remembering more than that. We moved out of my grandparents' house when I was seven and, at that time, my worry accelerated from a passenger (somatic symptoms including both stomachaches and headaches) to a driver (a worry that filled my mind with ideas on an endless loop, so many ideas related to bad guys and death and being left alone that they sometimes quite literally took my breath away). I started putting butter knives under my bed to protect my mom. I was never really concerned about protecting myself; somehow I always knew I would make it out okay. She, though, needed the protection only an underweight eight-year-old girl plagued with fear and holding a butter knife can offer.

I still use that proverbial dull and essentially useless weapon to protect people I love; only now it comes in the form of plans, order, and control.

It seems my body has partnered with anxiety to take this planning to a new level. All these doctor appointments for some kind of mysterious health problem distract me even more, keeping me from the proverbial bottom of the ocean floor, violently pushing me up to the surface anytime I get too close, leaving me gasping for air.

A bully preys on the weak, the fearful, the vulnerable. A bully knows not to mess with kids who are confident and self-assured because those kids will see right through the farce. "Who do you think you are?" they'd ask; then when the bully couldn't prove he was, in fact, the toughest kid on the block, those kids would laugh at him and walk away. *Far better*, the bully reasons, *to find someone who wouldn't dare challenge me.*

And so the bully, in my case, Fear, fueled by its cousin, Anxiety, goes on the hunt for the sensitive child, the one who brings a bird with a broken wing home so that her grandma can try to mend it with popsicle sticks and yarn. The one who brings stray dogs and cats home, tempting them with treats, only to say, "I don't know why, but this sweet dog/cat just kept following me. I think that's a sign we're meant to be a family!" Fear sought out this soft heart because he knew this heart could be controlled. The owner of this heart would melt the instant she felt Fear's hot breath in her face, warning her to know her place. Fear picked the one most prone to worry, the one most sensitive to emotional upset, the one who loves so deeply the mere thought of her most beloved hurt makes her reel out of control.

Fear and its cousin, Anxiety, chose me. I worry they will choose my sons, as well. They are sensitive like me and, even at their young age, they have a remarkable capacity for empathy and feeling things deeply. But my kids? They seem to be so braver and wiser than I ever was, maybe even more than I am to this day.

Tommy came in from playing one afternoon after I had just a fight with Craig.

"What's wrong, Mommy?" he asked.

"Nothing, honey, I'm fine," I lied. A three year old child does not need to bear the weight of his mother's pain.

"Mommy, you're lying. I can tell something's wrong because your eyebrows are all squished together."

Tommy-Empath, Same-Same. His laser focus on the truth, not only to spot it but also to feel it, put up a mirror that showed me a not-so-flattering reflection of myself. What was I teaching my child about honoring his feelings, about sharing those feelings, about letting someone in to love you when you're hurting?

"You're right, Tommy," I said. "I'm not telling the truth. I feel kind of sad, actually."

"It's ok, Mommy. I feel sad sometimes too. I get worried like you too. When I feel that way, you give me a hug. Do you want a hug too?"

A few days later I got a similar insight into Jackson's wisdom. While he is equally intuitive, he didn't yet have the capacity to articulate his worries. His propensity to internalize hurt had me worried recently when he announced that he wanted to paint his nails like me. Not wanting to squelch his creative expression ("One color for every fingernail, Mom!") I also knew not all of his fellow first-graders would be hip to his new vibe and that toxic masculinity that still, in this day and age, rears its head on the playground, even among six year olds. I wanted him to learn how to better share his feelings, not learn how to hide them more effectively.

I agreed, but only on the condition I could prepare him for what may come. Anticipatory planning through potential disaster is a trademark skill of mine (your greatest asset is your greatest liability, as they say, and anxiety is no different), so I thought I could let this go if we rehearsed a few scenarios. Conceding, Craig did the painting while I did the talking.

"Do you know any other boys who wear nail polish at school?"

"No," he said, beaming at the sparkly turquoise that was going on his index finger.

"I don't know any either, so I'm thinking you are going to be the coolest boy there, don't you?"

"YES!" Here comes the neon orange.

"Some families think some things are for girls and some things are for boys, so you may hear someone say, 'Nail polish is for girls,'" I continued.

"Well, that's stupid. That's like saying sports are for boys." On goes a shade of green.

"Right, so here's the thing: if someone says that to you, that thing about the nail polish being for girls, what might you say?"

Here comes purple. "I'd say, 'You're just jealous your mom and dad don't let you do what you want.'"

"Cool. Anything else, if they keep bugging you I mean?"

And finally, bright red. "I'd say, 'You're stupid,' and then go play soccer with my friends. Really Mom, is this such a big deal?" My husband laughed and got some nail polish on Jackson's thumb. "Cool! Now it looks like someone tried to cut my hand off!"

I laughed and cried simultaneously, that thing you do as a parent when you realize just how extraordinary your children are.

After having Mario for a few months we had developed a rhythm together, walking twice a day, about three miles each time. While Officer Sharon told me he was about three years old, the vet thinks he's closer to one. The more comfortable he's gotten at home, the more that puppy has been revealing himself. I like my shoes. And my headphones. And my glasses. Turns out he does too, most of all how they feel in his mouth after he's chewed through them. And so we walk, a lot, to try to help him put that energy to less destructive use.

Recently I've tried to take different routes; I tend to be a find-the-route-you-like-and-stick-with-it kind of girl, in life and in dog walking, so recently I thought I'd push out of my box a little bit and try to discover some new ways around the neighborhood.

I've found some amazing places on my dog walking travels. Beautiful, still lagoons with families of ducks, pairs of loons, and solitary egrets; I even happened upon the most unusual creature who looks as if he is a combination chicken and duck, whom I now affectionately call, "Chuck." I've also had the pleasure of identifying patterns that some of the ocean birds follow. When the tide is low, for example, an enormous flock of pelicans come to feast; when the tide is high seagulls come calling, diving in and out of the water seeming only to mew at one another, as if they are shouting a series of expletives. It's been a peaceful time for me, and with the exception of the foul-mouthed seagulls, a quiet place for me to gather my thoughts at the beginning and end of each day.

While pleased with my mix-of-path options, I realized something yesterday: no matter where I go when I walk the dog, I always take the concrete path. My shoes are new, the concrete path ensured they'd stay clean. The concrete path is smooth, no unexpected bumps or jagged edges to surprise me or trip me up; on the concrete path I can look forward, know what's ahead, feel secure in where I'm going and how I'm getting there. I know the people on the concrete paths, politely nodding their heads "Good Morning" or "Good Evening" to me as I pass. The concrete path is stable, structured, well understood.

Yesterday was a pretty typical Bay Area summer morning: cold, foggy, misty. The wind was whipping and I was freezing. Why do I always anticipate a warmer situation than what I know will inevitably await? It's summer, it *should* be warm. And in the Bay Area where I've lived my whole entire life, I know summer mornings are never warm. What should be vs. what is. I hate "shoulds," but I always seem to pick them.

Normally under these conditions I would head for one of the lagoons where the paths are protected, some even by a canopy of trees that provides extra shelter from the cold. As I moved toward the lagoon, I felt the leash tug the other way as Mario had a different plan. He had caught a glimpse of a squirrel in the other direction and raced after it, dragging me behind.

Once I got a handle on him (and myself) I realized that maybe the cold was okay. I'd walk fast, I thought, and the cool air may clear my head. Walking down the concrete path near the shore-line I scanned to the right to see if I could see the city, but it was no use—too foggy. On my scan back, however, I noticed some-thing. The concrete path was something like thirty feet from the water. What was I doing so far away from something so beautiful? I made an uncharacteristically impulsive decision: new shoes be damned, I headed for the dirt path that ran directly along the shore.

The dirt path is the opposite of the concrete path: its sides me-ander rather than follow a smooth line; the ground is uneven, cov-ered with rocks jutting up from nowhere, holes that are home to ground squirrels, weeds with mossy spider legs found in random clusters and clumps. At high tide you could reach out and touch the water from the dirt path; at low tide the algae covered rocks, usually hidden by the glorious San Francisco Bay, are exposed, showing the not so pretty underbelly of what resides just under the surface.

Because the dirt path is so close to the water, the wind is stron-ger, and the cold is colder. Walking on the dirt path is unpredict-able, I can't look ahead for fear of falling on my face; I can look out to the water and the world around me sometimes, but mostly I must concentrate on the path below me; it forces me to pay atten-tion to exactly where I am, clear and conscious of the present step instead of focused on the future.

The dirt path allows me to take in my surroundings with sens-es other than my eyes: I can feel it, smell it, taste it, hear it—in fact it comes to me in ways I never knew were there.

Although a more exhilarating walk, I wasn't sure I'd walk that dirt path again anytime soon. By the time we got home, I was dirty, the dog was dirty, and the squirrels that had been popping in and out of their holes left me feeling kind of freaked out (especially given Mario's unrelenting prey drive that meant at any time I might see my arm dangling behind him as he ran after one of those squirrels, having been pulled clean out from the socket).

But when I got up this morning, I realized I needed that path. In an attempt to stabilize the precariousness of my youth, I created an adulthood marked exclusively by structure and forward motion. Graduate from high school, go to college, start a career at 22, get married at 25, have a baby at 30, have a second baby at 33. It was a plan that I made as a teenager and followed as an adult as if my life depended on it. Now, though? Now I long for a path that will show me how to walk unhindered by the compulsion that leads me to that never-attainable place called "perfection," a place that has me living in the future, a place that robs me of my present.

So I will walk the dirt path again today, not because I know my surroundings, but because I trust myself. What I don't yet know about myself cannot be found on the steady, trustworthy concrete path; I must push to the dirt path because only out of a mess can true understanding be born. Only on the dirt path will I learn about the things that will make me strong, learning how to navigate challenges instead of avoiding them, so I don't have to fear the unknown anymore. I must face that path and do so with courage, knowing that life itself is dirty and bumpy and unpredictable.

Some days I will need the concrete path, and that's okay. Some days I will feel nervous and only my dog will give me the courage I need to move to the dirt path, and that's okay too. Over time those fears will quiet and I will forge ahead, head held high, and squirrels be damned.

Until that day comes, I'll just be sure I take my dog.

Nicole Lusiani

Take Responsibility

"Each of us will have to make the choices
that allow us to be the largest versions
of ourselves."

– Julia Alvarez

The summer before last I had a panic attack. This wasn't your garden-variety moment of stress—it was a chest tightening, left arm searing, I can't breathe and I think I'm going to die panic attack that put me in the emergency room of the local hospital.

We were on vacation, the boys were napping, Craig and I were reading on the back porch when, out of nowhere, I was seized by what I thought must be a heart attack. My husband dragged the kids out of bed as the advice nurse suggested we get to the hospital "with all due speed." And speed we did.

Impressively calm, Craig dropped me off at the emergency room's entrance as he parked the car, keeping our children focused on the understanding that Mommy was feeling yucky and needed to check in with a doctor. Meanwhile I wasn't three steps in the door before I was rushed into the back, stripped of my shirt, and hooked up to what felt like ten different machines.

Within about fifteen minutes the rush that had greeted me at the door had slowed considerably as had the number of staff members attending to my health. A nurse had put something in my IV "to help me relax." I didn't think I was any more stressed out than any other thirty-something who likely just had a heart attack. Regardless, the drug put me in a warm bath kind of state, and I felt a strange, but huge, sense of relief.

A doctor dressed in shorts and a tank top under her white coat came through the door, her flip-flops flipped and flopped as she looked through my chart.

"How long have you struggled with anxiety?" she asked.

"Struggled with what?" I was perplexed. "Anxiety?" In my bath-like state I wasn't sure I had heard her correctly.

"Yes, anxiety. You had one doozy of a panic attack just now."

A "doozy?" A flip-flop wearing doctor just used the word "doozy?" I must admit I had a moment of thinking perhaps I had died and this was my transition to heaven. Dramatic? Yes, I am prone to the dramatics. In my defense, however, I was also pretty heavily drugged.

"I thought I had a heart attack," I replied, still terribly confused.

"The signs are remarkably similar," she replied, as a nurse who I hadn't seen came in and started ripping those little sticky circles off my chest. As I cringed, she continued.

"You'd be surprised how often we see it up here. A person's body relaxes and all the worries her subconscious was holding begin to surface. A panic attack can occur as a result and, when it's severe like yours, it resembles a heart attack so closely that we go into cardiac arrest protocol. Thankfully, you don't have a heart condition; you only have anxiety."

Only anxiety. I'm not relieved.

Just after my doctor delivered this "good" news, the nurse untied my gown and started to rip those little round discs from my back, clearly having no regard for the fact that I'm Italian and have a bit more body hair than the average white girl. I was considering her good fortune that I was medicated and couldn't readily swing my fists at her when I heard Craig and the kids come through the door.

"Do you still feel yucky, Mommy?" Tommy asked.

"A little bit, honey, but I'm okay," I lied.

I didn't have a heart attack. I was healthy. It was only anxiety. I should have been okay.

The truth? I was not okay.

***

In the office of my acupuncturist a few weeks later, I recounted the story of the heart/panic attack. She responded quite simply, "If you don't do your work to get to the root of what's bothering you, all I'm doing is taking your money."

***

Here I am now, over a year since the aforementioned panic attack, holding my arm and trying to catch my breath. This time, I know it's not a heart attack. I also know that I can't run from it anymore. My acupuncturist's words came to me as immediately as the memory of the nurse ripping off the EKG wires.

If I don't get a handle on my life, I will continue to run on the hamster wheel toward nowhere. Only how can I get a handle on my life when I can't even manage to breathe?

I went to my doctor after losing more than ten pounds in a matter of a few weeks and experiencing the chest tightening, breath-seizing anxiety no longer waits a year between visits. It seemed to come calling every day about 4:30, an hour before Craig gets home from work. It took me too long to make this appointment; truth be told I only did it when the pain of the situation finally outweighed the payoff for ignoring it.

Within five minutes of being on that crinkly paper, shifting to find a comfortable place on the inside as much as the outside, I broke down sobbing. I told the doctor everything: I've worked my whole life to get where I am and now that I am here, I can't breathe. I feel like I'm suffocating in my own home. I've spent the last two years busying myself with work and raising my children and a hundred other things, all so I don't have to face the fact my marriage is failing.

"I can't do it anymore. Sometimes Craig is kind and loving, other times he's terribly hurtful. I'm on his roller coaster all the time and I can't find my own gravity. My children are feeling the effects of the stress in my house and their hurt hurts me more than anything else. I created this life for them, so they'll have a stable family and a home and a nice neighborhood and good schools. I'm killing myself to achieve and accomplish, to be and do better, so they can be whoever they were created to be and do whatever their dreams call them to do. I'm proud of myself. I'm proud of myself but I'm afraid. I'm afraid and I just can't catch my breath..."

An hour later I walked out of my doctor's office with a list of therapists, two prescriptions for anxiety medications, and a hug. Sometimes I think that woman saved my life.

The dog. The quiet. The dirt path. The doctor. Small, sequential steps toward my ability to create space between me and the voices that take my breath away. None of those things happened without the other, each an interlocking wheel moving me inward, away from the noise of my life and closer to the truth of myself.

What happens if the truth of myself doesn't match the reality of my life?

In what was becoming all too common an experience, I walked the dog this morning with a lot on my mind. I walked across the street, through the park, and out toward the water. I got to the street I needed to cross to get to the dirt path by the water and I didn't remember really even leaving the front porch, let alone walking the five minutes it took to get to my then current position. I shook my head because it all kind of reminded me of the last several years.

We walked along the water, Mario and me, listening to music. The title of this particular mix indicated I wasn't going to have to think much, just listen and enjoy it. Listen and enjoy it, I did; but I also did some thinking, a lot of it. Many things on my mind as I walked along the path, watching the water lap, noticing the grey fog tinged with pink, looking at the few miles of water between me and arguably one of the most beautiful cities in the world.

I soon realized that Mario was no longer in front of me. I looked back along the black rope of his leash and found him standing on top of a bench. On these benches I often see people sitting, taking in the sights, contemplating their lives, struggling or celebrating, but always deep in thought. Thankfully, on this particular bench (and this early in the morning) there were no people. There was, however, an odd collection of items left behind by the evening prior's inhabitants: a large rock, a 4 x 4 wood block, and a stick.

Mario was standing atop this bench working with all his fortitude to pick up the rock. He tried with his mouth, over and over different angles each time, to no avail. Then, he tried with his paws—if he could just get the right angle maybe he could sweep it up and off the bench. He spent several minutes working at this rock; finally, he had to surrender to the reality that, without the aid of opposable thumbs, the rock and he could not move forward together.

Instead of jumping down in despair, he moved on. When others would quit, Mario just changed course. He decided to take on the block. Surely he could make this happen. It was smaller, lighter, all around more manageable. He tried with all his might to get a hold of it. At one point he knocked it off the bench and jumped after it. "Success!" he must have thought as his whole body wagged in delight. Sadly, the block hit the ground before he could catch it. He gnawed it for a while and then, just as before, recognized it was just too big for him to manage.

Unlike me, in the battle between what should be and what is, Mario consistently chooses the latter. He happily leapt back up to the bench, pushed the stick around a bit with his nose, and then picked it up. With glee he jumped off the bench with this stick in his mouth; joyfully shaking his head he danced around me, a celebration in the dog form of "I did it!"

I laughed. I laughed and laughed and laughed. That morning, I learned more from my dog than perhaps anyone else in my life.

When an obstacle exists, jump up to tackle it. Aim big, but if that doesn't work, just shift course. A failure would be jumping off the bench. To take on the next available obstacle is just plain logical. If that one is also insurmountable, there's a lesson there too: don't take on more than you can. Do the best you can with what you know and be proud that you are doing it at all. Don't dwell in what should be possible; delight in what is possible. You may need tools you don't yet have to deal with life's bigger challenges; that's okay, because that's exactly the way things are supposed to be in this very moment, the only moment we are ever guaranteed.

In Mario's case, he'll need someone to teach him to walk upright and grow those opposable thumbs before he can tackle that rock. Something tells me the tools I need won't be quite that difficult to find.

Until then, I just need to pick up the damn stick.

When I was younger, I would lie in bed at night and plan. Unlike many other little girls, I wasn't planning my emergence as an actress or constructing a plan to be the first female president; what I was planning was my survival. A robber comes into our apartment, what do I do? My mom loses her job, what do I do? I fail seventh grade math, what do I do? Almost every night I would encounter different worries in my head and the way I talked myself out of them was to plan my way through them. Planning my survival had become my survival.

This worry-strategize-relax way of being followed me into adulthood, only here the worries are much bigger than they once were: if Jackson gets cancer, where do I take him to get the best possible care? If I hear the overpass crumbling above me, how do I get to Tommy in the back seat so that at least he dies in my arms? As a child worrying about a parent, my logic could often override my emotion; but when it's the other way around no amount of logic and planning could ever create a scenario where I would be okay.

Looking back, it's clear I've always had issues with anxiety; the difference is that, before, I thought I could manage it. That's the thing, though. Once you think you have a lifelong issue "managed," it finds a new way to create havoc.

It was three years ago when I realized what I thought was a tendency toward worry was actually much more serious. Seven months pregnant with Tommy, we put Jackson to bed and settled in for a "date night," the only way a pregnant woman with a pre-schooler often can: it was movie night and on tap that night was the movie Ray. Not far into the movie young Ray Charles watched his brother drown, paralyzed by his inability to save him.

I went into hysterics. I couldn't breathe, I couldn't speak, I could only sob. My husband paused the movie and looked at me with a mixed look on his face that asked both, "Are you okay?" and "What the hell is wrong with you?" After a few minutes I found my composure and attributed the reaction to hormones and my usual oversensitivity to other people's heartache. What I was really doing with that explanation was covering over the depths of my worry with a heavier serving of denial than usual.

From that point forward my internal monologue went into overdrive. I couldn't plan my way out of grief at the potential loss of one of my children, but I sure could plan my days, my lists, my reactions to others... you name it, I tried to manage it.

When I started trying to manage the feelings and behaviors of others, it created significant stress, particularly in my marriage. My issues clashed terribly with Craig's and we couldn't seem to string together more than a day or two without an argument. Everything was a struggle and, while I should have been living happily with all the things and relationships I'd worked so hard to cultivate, I actually felt a dull ache of emptiness that weighed me down in the worst sort of way.

Unable to figure out the what or why of our problems, Craig and I each turned inward and lost connection more every day. This, of course, created more anxiety which manifested in even more attempts to control anything I could because I couldn't face the one thing I couldn't control: my life.

Just as I know the path of a lesson gets longer the longer it takes to learn it, I also know when I try to ignore that lesson, the message gets sent more forcefully. I know this, I've lived it. Again. And again.

Just after Tommy's first birthday, I got the chance to learn a lesson about truth and courage from my marriage, once again. After years of steeling through, barely keeping our heads above water raising babies and going to graduate school and paying our mortgage and living within a marriage that was not allowing either of us to be truly free, Craig and I came to a point of reckoning from which we could not return. He came to me one night, sat down with me on our bed, took a deep breath, and shared that he had been unfaithful to me. In the week to come, as I came to terms with my denial and forced many questions out of my mouth that I'd never had the courage to ask, I learned that it was not just one time.

In the moment, however, before the courage fueled by rage arrived in the days to come, I felt my heart unravel. My chest heaved as heat raced up my neck and into my scalp. It was a heat I had never known before, one that brought me to the ground and one that felt like it just might explode my insides. All of the years of trying to figure out his rules so he wouldn't get enraged, all of the times I threw myself in between him and our kids when he came down too hard on them, all of things I let go to keep peace, all the decisions I made sacrificing myself to the point I didn't even know what made me happy anymore…it lit a fire in me that burned up every last bit of denial.

In the days and weeks that followed, I came to understand that Craig's betrayal catalyzed this emotional devastation, but, in truth, the roots of destruction could be found in tatters alongside the years of poor decisions both of us had made. Untruths on both sides, pain and fear too. There's more than one way to be unfaithful to a partner and the reality is we made our way to this place together. Craig wanted to work together to build a new us and, after two heart-wrenching months, I agreed.

I could have taken the opportunity to acknowledge my anxiety and work toward surrendering my need to control everything. I could have fought against the role of victim, to battle through the truth of what got us there, to do the hard work it really takes to heal from complete heartbreak and emerge on the other side a warrior, better for the pain and better for the journey.

I did none of those things.

I just wanted to hold my family together, to protect my children and myself, and to hold on to my understanding of what success was. I knew Craig's choices had little to do with me, personally; I knew I was strong and smart, attractive and desirable, loving and compassionate. I knew I had a role in creating his pain, and I also knew his decision to manifest that pain in the form of varying degrees of betrayal had very little to do with me.

Still, it hurt. It hurt so badly. Looking back, I think what actually scared me the most was that I couldn't control him; I could only control me. That's logical and even healthy in certain contexts;

in mine, however, it was neither. It just fed an irrational belief that if I changed me, maybe he wouldn't betray me again.

Instead of doing the hard work of self-healing that this lesson was begging me to do, I side-stepped it and got back on that circular path, retreating further inward toward self-management. My mission was clear: I was strong; I should be able to rise above and keep my family together. If it happened again, the fact that I did everything possible would be my ticket to both redemption and divorce. I thought it was noble, I thought it was right; I thought I was being a better person by overcoming adversity for the good of the whole. Unbeknownst to me, I would fall into an unceasing compulsion to control once again.

Mario picked up the stick that day out by the water because he recognized the block was out of reach for him. He changed course to deal with what was instead of what should be.

It would take me a few more years to learn that lesson.

I found myself talking to an old friend today. An old boyfriend, actually. Although I don't know if you could technically call him a "boyfriend" because we never went out on a real date. We went on walks and talked a lot and spent a fair amount of time making out. We were only 18 years old, so I suppose all that just might make him a boyfriend.

I don't remember meeting him; my first memory isn't of him, it's of us together, walking across the lawn to my residence hall. He was telling a story and I was laughing. On the way up to my room to finish talking and have some snacks from the mini-fridge I shared with my roommate, I felt the weight of his stare on the back of my head as I reached over to push the number three in the elevator. I was wearing a coral colored t-shirt, khaki shorts, and my hair was in a ponytail, tied up with a scarf from the 1970s that I had found in my mom's drawer the summer before. I could feel in his stare that he thought I was pretty; when I turned around, I could see in the way he looked at me that he thought I was smart. I knew from the way he smiled that both of those things made him a little nervous. I could see him. And he could see me.

Perhaps it was that we shared the same cultural and religious heritage. Or that we both loved the written word. Or that we each struggled against the same God and the decisions He made on our behalf without our consent. Likely all three.

We spent a lot of time together those first two months of school; then, as quickly as he came, he was gone. Gone due to the fear of our connection, or to the endless supply of beer, or maybe to the next smart, pretty girl who he charmed into loving him.

I was hurt at first but bounced back quickly. Ours was not a deeply devoted kind of young love; it was more of a knowing. It was a kind of knowing that safely transitioned us away from our familial home into the new home of college and friends and clean slates we called young adulthood. No matter his antics in the months and years that followed—and there were several—this knowing remained. We knew that in one another, we had a home.

The night of graduation we somehow ended up together toward the middle of the night. We had been celebrating with friends and saw each other in the common area between all the senior townhouses. Although I don't remember the details, I assume we made arrangements to meet several hours later. Just like old times, we walked and talked, laughed and made-out. And then we parted ways, closing our four years of college much as we opened them: in a brief but clear knowing of one another.

And that was that. Although I had seen him once a few years later, we hadn't kept in touch. I had no idea where he was or what he was doing. I hadn't even given him much thought since May of 1994.

Until today.

This unusually warm summer morning I opened Facebook to find a note in my inbox from him. In a sweet and genuinely excited tone he expressed happiness to have come across my name in the

"People you may Know" section of his page. As soon as I accepted his friend request, he popped up in the chat area, and there he and I remained for the better part of the day. In the spaces between me caring for my kids and him tending to his job, we caught up on life events, and then delved deeper into life stories. At first I thought it was just the relative anonymity of chatting online that allowed me to open up in all sorts of ways, telling him about my joys and my sadness. I found it so intimate it scared me a little bit.

Then I thought about that day in the elevator, the details of which I remember more clearly than most other memories. That recognition. I felt it again. I felt what it feels like to have someone know me, know what I mean, what I need, who I am… all without having to explain it. He knew me then. Almost two decades later, he still does.

I couldn't help but think of Craig, who I lived with every day, and I wondered if he ever really knew me at all. Of course he knew me, but I mean knew me, with no need to go looking for reasons to be offended because in my heart, he could see and hear and feel his own.

Craig didn't know me like that. I don't know if he ever did. I don't know if he ever will.

My doctor said that within a few weeks of taking the medication I would find this space, the space where I'd still feel anxious but where the anxiety would be "blunted" and, therefore, not so debilitating. I wasn't sure what she meant until recently, but she was exactly right. I'm still upset, I'm still anxious, but the frantic and frightening instinct of fight, flight, or freeze is tempered enough that I can almost think straight.

A sense of peace was emerging. It wasn't between Craig and me, it was just within me.

This is coming along with the help of counseling, my own and ours, as a couple. Craig and I started counseling two years ago when our bottom dropped out. It helped at first, allowing me a deep sense of validation while also calling on me to learn how I might be contributing to our challenges. I learned a lot then; now, however, counseling was feeling like an exercise in futility.

"Wait, I thought everything was better?" is a question I often get when I share with others what's happening in my marriage. "I don't understand," they continue, "from the outside it looks like things *should* be just *fine.*"

"Maybe it should be fine," I reply, "but it's not."

Eleven years we've been married. Eleven years of beautiful and brutal moments. The brutal ones are coming more regularly for me now, maybe because I'm seeing what is rather than what should be. I see the intensity of his mood swings, I hear the crack of his criticism, and I feel the weight of both bearing down in my body. The resentment, the anger, the relentlessness of all of it—all of it, not just what he created, but also what I've created, and what we've created—I refuse to be party to it anymore.

Maybe things *should be fine*. But they're not.

Too many years of unhealed wounds have left us with scar tissue, scar tissue that has frozen us in the brutal times so acutely that not even the beautiful times can be the balm they once were.

Maybe things should be fine. But they're not.

Craig wants to work hard toward our healing; I just want to work on my own. I don't want him to be hurt, but the fact he is upset, even the fact he is upset with me, no longer rings the alarm bell for me. That damned bell rang so loud and so often for so many years that I finally just found the switch and turned it off. As liberating as that is, I can't deny the detachment that's come with it as, at least in this moment, I find myself intolerant of anyone's pain beyond my own.

Craig thinks I'm being selfish; I think others feel the same. Something I've lost in recent weeks is the pervasive and painful burden that was my incessant worry about what other people think and feel. Other people have had my attention, focus, and energy for too long. I'm rewriting my script and that's long overdue.

I wish I had had the foresight to find a balance between self-care and the care of others years ago, but I didn't and now here we all are, sitting deep in the truth of what we have allowed our lives to become: a deeply painful place made bearable by the simple fact it's true.

It's the end of a very emotional weekend. Year twelve of an annual retreat with my personal and professional mentors reminds me that the love of good friends is simply and profoundly an extension of God's love.

When I came into the cabin a few days ago, I could see the worry in their eyes. I have lost more than twenty pounds, my eyes have deep circles, my skin is pale, and my hair is dull. I was in the last car to arrive, just one other and me who couldn't manage more than one day off work, so we drove up after school. The moment I walked in they put their wine glasses down and jumped to their feet to embrace me. It was more than clear that, before my arrival, I had been a topic of conversation. While I may have bristled with worry about that thought a year ago, at that moment I felt both humbled and deeply grateful.

It warms me, their concern. I am loved and, if only for this weekend, I have to take care of nothing and no one but myself. Meals are made, wine is poured, tears are shed, stories are shared. They took me in their collective arms where I was held in the greatest of care. They know the stories of two years ago but thought, like so many others, that Craig and I had healed and moved on; I can't blame them for not understanding what I barely understood myself. Almost all of them attended my wedding; now they bear witness to what may be the end of my marriage.

These women range in age thirty years. In our eleven years coming to majestic Yosemite, we have seen each other plan weddings, call off weddings, buy houses, have babies, build schools, change schools, retire, and lose spouses to untimely deaths. We started coming to this cabin over a decade ago as women who taught together, bonded by the love of our students and the profession to which we had dedicated our lives; we keep coming as women bonded through all of life's joys and sorrows, having been through so many of them together.

Tovi, a woman with whom I was a first year teacher who has a love for all things fun and spiritual in equal measure, brought a book with her this weekend about Archangel Michael. I always believed in angels, but this book had "that" look: the one that says you can only buy it in a store full of incense and crystals with a mysterious woman behind the counter, wearing out the words "universe" and "spirit."

She handed it to me.

"Are you kidding me with this?" I mocked.

She looked at me with raised eyebrows and a small tip of the head that said, "Are you kidding me by asking that?"

She had a point. I was wrecked. Who was I to mock her move toward an ever expanding understanding of spirituality? If there was anything I needed, it was an angel, so I picked it up. When I finished two hours later my mind reeled. If I ever felt a divine connection with something I read, it was then.

The direct messages were uncanny given all things I needed to do, serving more as a reminder than new information. I needed to cut the cords of fear that were strangling my breath and, in their place, build the cords of love that breathe in life. Moreover, the book was very clear about the importance of asking for help. It claimed that free will forbade the sending of answers unless someone asked. But asking for help is not what I do; I'm the person who can get it done on her own, a lone wolf, a noble pioneer, a rugged individualist.

Who the hell am I kidding?

So ask, I did. I put down that book, put on my earphones, went to my computer and typed. Looking back, I think it may seem a little crazy; even in the moment I felt a little crazy. I still feel a little crazy. I don't know if it was Michael talking back to me or just me getting quiet enough to hear the answers I already knew—maybe both. All I know is, it was a profound experience that left me with two answers.

Feel the fear and move on through.

***

Dear Michael,

First let me acknowledge I feel like a crazy person. I'm writing a letter to an angel with the idea you might write back. I think I may have lost my mind for real.

That said, let me follow the directions and say this: Michael, I need you to help me with some answers. If you can't, if I'm not ready, please tell me that too. I need guidance.

I'm here.

Whoa. Are you me or are you, you? I thought this was supposed to be an "I talk, you listen, then you answer" kind of situation. I wasn't counting on INTERACTION.

Sounds like your perception of the way things should be gets in the way of the truth. How's that working for you?

Not well, thanks. There's so much to ask, I almost don't even know where to start.

Just start.

Um, okay. First, let me ask you and Raphael to help me release the metaphysical cause for my physical discomfort.

No, first, drop the act. That book got you to me, now stop trying to follow directions and just follow your heart.

My back hurts.

Okay, describe it to me.

The tension across my upper back, into my shoulders, up my neck, around my ear, and through the left side of my face. Where is it coming from and why?

The tension is the burden you carry. The worry and the fear—it's a lack of faith and lack of surrender.

Where does that tension come from?

Within. It doesn't exist beyond what you make of it. I've told you already: you make your own reality. You choose it every day.

So it's a simple choice? I either carry it or I don't?

Mostly, yes. Sometimes you need help to release into a more positive reality. That's where Raphael and I come in. We're here to help you let it go. Give it to us; we'll carry it for you. We'll give it to God and He will gladly take it. Your choice to take it on yourself is not only hurting you, it's a sign of your arrogance.

I know I tend to think I can handle most things on my own. I take pride in it. I take comfort in it. I rely on it. Sometimes it even plays into how I treat others and my expectations of them.

Sometimes? How do you think you got into this mess?

Okay, most times. Are you some kind of smart-ass in addition to being an angel?

Yes. And you're welcome. You need to release your hold on your life and live in the faith you say you have.

I do have faith. I feel it so strongly; it's so real for me—especially in walking the dog and in being in connection with old friends. They have opened the door to an even deeper faith than I even knew I had.

Then walk through the door, my friend. They opened it with my guidance. Your charge is to move your feet.

How do I know which direction to go once I get through the door?

You'll know. Trust me, trust yourself. You are worthy of our love, yours and mine and all those you love and who love you. We will clear your path if you only have the faith to walk through the door.

So, this door, is it out of my marriage or into it?

Don't you know?

No, I don't. That's why I'm asking you.

Yes you do. That's why you are asking me.

I think it's a door out. But I'm not sure.

Why are you not sure?

Because I'm afraid. And I love him. And I love our family.

I know. That's why I'm here.

Can you help me cut the cords of fear? I don't know if I can do it myself.

What are you afraid of?

Making the wrong decision. He is a good man. He is kind and loving and an fantastic father. Our marriage was so troubled, but now it seems like something has shifted. I've changed, he seems to be changing. Maybe it could get better?

You have nothing to fear except the fear you create yourself. I can cut this cord of fear with you, but unless you release the need to live in fear you will only create more cords for yourself.

So you are saying you won't enable me?

Yep. Stop trying to control everything. You have to have open hands to receive what is possible. Let it be.

Let me pause again to say thank you. Thank you for these amazing people I'm here with, for everything. I feel so blessed in so many ways. It almost doesn't seem fair.

It's your birthright. I've come to you like I will come to anyone who needs me and asks for help. People need to allow themselves to be open, in whatever small way they can manage. They'll get there; those are their journeys—you stay focused on yours.

Right.

I told you I couldn't and wouldn't help you release your fear until you were clear that you were done needing it. For your whole life, fear has been your crutch. I know you don't need it anymore; doesn't seem you know that yet.

Without fear, what will I do? It protects me, right?

No, I do. God does. Your ancestors do. Fear blocks us out. But you've convinced yourself you need to maintain control, that you need to keep everything in order. That's the whole point. Releasing the fear will release your control, or perceived control. It's really not the fear you are afraid of releasing, it's the control.

I'm tired of trying to keep everything together. I'm tired of being strong. I'm tired of trying to be perfect. I can't do it anymore. I don't want to do it anymore.

Then stop.

It's not that easy.

I never said it was easy. I said anything valuable and necessary is worth fighting for.

So, do I fight for my marriage or do I fight for my independence?

84

And, again, I say, you struggle by your own choice. Stop. Stop struggling, stop fighting, stop worrying. Just be quiet and still and listen. Rest. Take a break and rest. I'm not going anywhere.

***

For the next day and a half, I slept. I woke up and spent four hours at the dining room table creating a vision board for my new life. It's a work of art, visually and spiritually.

I've never been so tired. And I've never been so clear.

Feel the Fear and Walk on Through

"Barn's burnt down—
Now I can see the moon."

- Masahide

I had to leave. If I stayed, we'd be done for good. If I left, if I did the work, I needed to do in a space that was only mine, a space untarnished by hurt, a space designed for the sole purpose of my healing; then and only then could I, maybe, find my way back home.

It was the single hardest thing I've ever done, telling Craig I had to leave. That is, until we had to tell our children. For a lifetime, I've carried the fear of abandoning them; the power of that fear manifested in exactly that moment.

Ironically, I got through it because of Craig. Last week I told our therapist I was going to move out and, after she took a deep breath and looked at us with great empathy, I asked her how to tell the kids. She worked with Craig and me to create a plan and we left her office feeling what can only be described as the deepest kind of empty any two humans can feel.

I was sobbing and Craig was equally, albeit more quietly, upset. He reached for my hand and said, "We're going to do this right. It'll be okay." More sobs came. How could I be doing this to my family?

Then again, how could I not?

"Mommy and Daddy are having a really hard time using our good words with each other," he said to our kids the following weekend. "We have been going to a doctor for some help and it still isn't working. Mommy feels like the best thing she can do is to take a break, like we ask you guys to do when you can't seem to treat each other properly. Does that make sense?"

"Yes. But, Mommy, where are you going?" Tommy asked me, speaking the fearful question to which both boys were clinging.

"I found a place just ten minutes from here," I explained. "You know how Daddy takes you to school every morning? He still will. And you know how I pick you up every afternoon? I still will. I'll pick you both up and we'll play, have dinner, and bath and bedtime. Then, instead of going to bed in mine and Daddy's room, I'll go to bed at my new sleeping place."

More questions ensued, both of us answering the best and most honestly we could with a forced tone of confidence. Confident was the last thing either one of us was but, for our children, we would do whatever it took to reassure them of our love for them and for each other. We do love each other. That's why I'm doing this, right? Trying to save myself so I could then join the fight to try to save my marriage?

A few days later, Mario and I sat on my garage sale couch in my "sleeping place." There in that tiny, cold apartment with a view of the town's only parking garage we sat in the kind of heavy silence that comes after a weighty decision.

I wasn't so sure I knew what I was doing, after all.

What I did know is, for the first time in months, I could breathe.

My mom tells a handful of stories about my great-grandmother. Sitting here in my half-unpacked tiny apartment, they all come to mind.

She wore a St. Christopher pendant around her neck. It was on a long chain, so the pendant always sat between her breasts. When my mom was little, she'd sit on Nonnina's lap and fish out St. Christopher from between those "giant boobies" and when it arrived in the palm of her hand it was always so warm. She'd put it to her cheek and Nonnina would hug her and all would be right with the world.

My parents were married in December of 1971. My mom was 21 years old. She worked tirelessly making her dress, the dresses for her bridesmaids, and coordinating the details of the wedding. One of those details was about candles for the altar.

When Nonnina heard this, she thought maybe she didn't understand. My mom explained her vision for a beautiful candle-lit altar for a winter evening wedding. Nonnina promptly told her there was no need for her to save seats for her and Nonno because they would never go to such a wedding. Heartbroken, my mom asked how that could possibly be?

Without missing a beat Nonnina insisted, "You just want a night wedding so you can get to bed faster!"

Three years later, my parents divorced. It was 1974, and at 23 years old with a two-year-old daughter, my mom was sure the choice was right, but she was still desperately afraid to tell Nonnina. If she wouldn't attend an evening wedding, what would she say to a divorce?

"*Non ho camminato nelle tue scarpe*," she said. At least this is what I think she said. I can only guess based on how the internet helped me write it because I don't have the language of my ancestors. My family chose assimilation as their path to their American dream. No language was passed to my parents with the exception of a few sayings that have carried forward over the years.

"*Non ho camminato nelle tue scarpe*." Loosely translated, I haven't walked a mile in your shoes.

This staunchly Catholic woman from the old country would not attend an evening wedding, but she also wouldn't judge her oldest granddaughter for leaving her husband. My mom said that when they hugged, had she still been a child, she would have gone looking for that St. Christopher pendant. As an adult, however, she was content with the warm embrace of her grandmother who loved her just as much that day as she did the day before.

***

When discussing the possibility of moving out, not one of the people I love the most initially supported the idea. They all had their own reasons, in common was their attempt to protect me from what might be worse times ahead. When I made the decision to do it anyway, however, all of the naysayers cast their worry and opinions aside and threw every bit of support they had behind me.

In recent days my loved ones have donated pots, pans, lamps, coat hooks, and everything else an apartment needs. My mom, aunt, and uncle moved me in. My best girls took me out to dinner. My email is flooded with daily messages of support. If I wasn't feeling so desperately sad, I'd be filled with gratitude. Come to think of it, even desperately sad I still am filled with gratitude.

I could never have imagined this would be me, yet here I am, my dog and me, alone in a tiny apartment contemplating just how we will live the rest of our lives. It strikes me that my mom may have very well felt the same way on the day she moved us into the bottom floor of my grandparents' house in 1974.

Non ho camminato nelle tue scarpe.

I've been thinking about two things: I am a people pleaser and I have good hair.

I know these two things don't seem to correlate, nor did they for me until relatively recently. I don't claim to be a beauty queen, but I do know I have great hair. It's thick and wavy and with a good haircut will look good with minimal effort. I had years in my early twenties where minimal effort would be a generous term, a direct departure from my teenage years when I focused so intently on my hair it turned into a bit of an obsession. By my late twenties, however, I had reached some balance.

I had also been married a couple years at that point, a period of time when my marriage was taking its first of many wrong turns. One of my memories of that time was not a big fight or major decision; instead was a conversation with my husband about my hair.

"Why does this one piece always fall in your face?" he asked as he brushed it away a little too harshly. "It's so irritating."

And with that, the two previously mentioned unrelated things braided together.

I snapped at him for being irritated with something so minor and he retreated. He didn't consider what was really bothering him and neither did I. I didn't consider why it hurt my feelings so much and neither did he. I don't even know if he remembers this conversation, perhaps to him it was that irrelevant or maybe just one of many similar interactions that foreshadowed the trouble to come. For me, though, it unconsciously devolved into something I needed to change in order to keep him happy.

From that day forward, I clipped my bangs to the side and never, ever, left the house without an extra hair clip in my pocket. That was ten years ago.

Today that same piece of hair fell in my face; instinctively I felt my pocket for an extra hair clip and then I stopped. I'm not orderly. I'm not logical. I'm not buttoned-up and polite. Sometimes I'm those things but more often than not I'm none of those things. Why would I expect myself to be something I'm not? What would I expect my hair to be something it isn't? Why can't I accept the whole me instead of just the parts of me that I think people will like?

This piece of hair is a part of who I am and if it needs to fall in my face, I'm going to damn well let it.

Wildflowers Don't Grow in Rows

"Wildflowers don't grow in rows.
And neither do I."

-Nicole Lusiani, *Nothing's Missing:
A Year of Reckoning, Release, and Remembering
Who I Am.*

I'm a Jane of many trades but a master in none. None, that is, except resistance. My body bears this out with the tension that runs down deep to my bones, creating what feels like steel cables up my spine and into my neck. I internalize everything, including the fact that I can't ever accept anything just as it is, not from myself and not from others. The manifestations of my resistance are pretty complex but the roots are not at all ambiguous. I am an expert at resistance because of my nemesis, *Should*.

Should has been around as long as I can remember. I was a very easy child to raise and to teach because I was so eager to please. While other kids might have needed to be yelled at or grounded, I just needed *Should*. *Should* would remind me what to do and how to do it and why. *Should* would knock any shred of rebellion out of me and hold me still. Quiet. Pretty. Obedient. A good girl. I never needed to learn to trust myself because I always had *Should* around to tell me what to do.

Lately I'm finding myself pretty pissed off at *Should* but I can't seem to shake her. Nothing ever just is when *Should* is in town. And *Should* is always in town.

I shouldn't feel that way.

I shouldn't be like that.

I shouldn't want to eat that.

I should be better at this.

In short, *Should* is a real asshole.

It feels so striking to me now because I am alone so much more often with my dog. While *Should* rules my world, only the present moment rules Mario's. This can be a danger (i.e., *I see those shoes, I must chew them*), but it is mostly a gift (*I see that lady, I must go smooch her*). Mario never resists a scrap of food or chasing a squirrel or barking at a potentially murderous mailman. And he never, ever resists an opportunity for joy or love, no matter when, where, or how they come.

What a beautiful frame of reference by which to live in the world. Sometimes he does get his heart broken but, because he lives so readily in the present moment, he has a remarkable resilience about him. (*I love my friend, she told me to go away and I'm sad. Oh! a toy! How wonderful!*).

And so it goes.

What I most envy is that Mario's inability to resist inherently leads him to trust his instincts. *Should* doesn't dwell in his town because he has no time or need for her. She can say all she wants but none of it matters because he trusts his own voice more than hers.

What kind of glorious liberation must this be?

Curious enough, since we've been together here in this apartment he has not chewed up one thing. He barely barks. He doesn't even chase his tail. He didn't need Should to tell him to make these changes because, at this point, his strongest instincts seem to be focused on protecting me. This is a place to keep safe, to keep quiet, to protect. *This is a place where my beloved needs me to chill out so she can take care of her business.*

He stands guard over me, this dog, not with *Should* or Fear or a butter knife, but with a grounded confidence in his instincts. Love and loyalty are his mechanisms of choice and, for the first time in my life, all alone in this tiny apartment, I really and truly feel safe.

Maybe I don't need *Should* to make decisions for me. Maybe I just need Mario to help me protect my space so I can make them for myself.

Like most mornings, I woke up early today. Sometimes it's a habit of a busy mind; when one thought creeps in the flood-gates open. This morning I inevitably fell from thinking about me to thinking about my family. I began a focused prayer to find what I needed to understand in order to have compassion for my husband, to understand him and accept him for who he is, not who I think he should be. But then the thoughts kicked back in. *How can I understand and accept him without letting go of myself even further? How do I hold true to who I am and what is acceptable to me, while still accepting a person for who they are?*

As I thought through the possibilities, I couldn't seem to find answers to these questions. It occurred to me that I'd been trying to find these answers for longer than I was ever consciously aware.

This struggle for control and identity really started long before Craig and I were married; if I were honest it probably started within me from the time I first started dating. I didn't have a healthy relationship model in my home; my parents divorced before I could walk, my mom never remarried, my dad did several times. As each of them struggled with how to face their own ghosts I allowed their internal conflicts to manifest as my own internal battle between what to give up for love and what to protect from it. This heartache has lived in me for as long as I can remember.

Among other things, I know I brought that struggle into my marriage. It was easy to dismiss in our early years together because we loved each other so much nothing else seemed to matter. About the time we started to wonder if, in fact, love could conquer all, we had our first child, and then our second. Deeply and quite naturally distracted, a whole new kind of love came into the world with our sons and nothing—nothing—else mattered.

I think my choice to burrow deeper into denial—a recurring if unconscious choice—is the source of my decades-long battle with my body. It started my senior year in high school. My hip, then my low back, then my pelvis. Many years later pregnancy exacerbated those chronic ailments. After my first dance with childbirth the pain reached up into my ear where, despite having no ear infection, I couldn't shake a painful sense of fullness; worse was the fact that every time I spoke, I heard myself in my own head. I felt like I was standing between two speakers and the words—incredibly loud, echoing words—were surging in one ear, through my head, and then back again.

This has taught me that, as much as children can heal your life's wounds, they also readily expose those wounds that still need attention. My propensity toward anxiety was never clearer than when I had my second son: how could I love two children at the same time? How could I keep them both safe? How could my attention be splintered even further to make sure they always stayed at the center of my heart as well as my decisions? All of this made my posture droop farther, my neck strain more, my ear echo louder. That was the second time I was invited to deal with my fear. And, for the second time, I declined the invitation.

Sadly, I am just recently connecting the dots among anxiety and control and fear and pain. Looking back now it feels so obvious, I guess I just wasn't ready to take responsibility for what I had grown to tolerate and the impact it was having on my health. Instead, I hid, burying myself in the worlds of my children. Over time that earplug-turned-echo wasn't just relaying my voice anymore: my breathing, my chewing, even my eyes moving back and forth, I could hear it all.

Everything, that is, except what it all was intended to make me hear.

I know now that it was God's way of saying, "Listen. Hear *yourself.*" Perhaps if I had allowed myself to be still and quiet, I may have heard that answer. I thought I was trying, but I wasn't. I just kept working, resisting my feelings through suppression and avoidance, busying myself with things that really didn't matter.

I think denial serves an important function: it lets you hide out until you are ready to deal. But healthy denial is designed to be temporary. Sooner or later we all have to emerge from our hiding place to face what was always waiting at the exit. When we do, truth be told, it's bigger, and the longer we wait, the bigger it gets. For almost twenty years I've been fighting a mysterious pain battle on the surface: endless and expensive appointments with doctors, neurologists, and chiropractors, all of them baffled by finding no source for my health issues. All of them baffled, that is, except for the acupuncturist who always knew that the answer could never come from anyone but me.

As I emerge from this den of denial, I'm faced with a mirror that shows me everything I haven't wanted to see. It's holding me responsible. And for the first time, I refuse to turn away.

"**H**ow do you know everything you've worked so hard for is really what you wanted and not just what you felt like you should want?"

A friend asked me this question a few days ago. We were talking about the possibility of me permanently leaving my husband, selling our house, effectively dismantling everything I've worked so hard to achieve. How could I do this? I asked. The focus of my adulthood has been to build this life for myself, how could I give it all up?

"Of course it is what I wanted!" I hastily replied, "I gave my children everything I wanted, growing up. I've lived the American Dream for God's sake. How could it not have been what I wanted?"

"Okay," she replied, as if I just ordered a pizza.

Okay, I considered.

Okay?

I wondered if I would ever feel okay again.

***

As dawn broke this morning, I delighted in the recognition of Autumn Day. Autumn Day is my unofficial day for when it seems to go from summer to autumn overnight. While yesterday was warm and sunny, overnight it stormed. The rain poured down and cleared the summer away; in its place are now cloudy skies and wind and fallen leaves. I love Autumn Day. It's a day that signals winter is coming, the time when what we don't need will die off and spring will bring new life.

New life. Just as the seasons, a caterpillar goes into the dark, turns to goo, struggles upon struggle to break free, and then emerges a butterfly. Everything is a mirror in this world for everything else. How we do one thing is how we do everything. And it's only when we go against our natural rhythms that we lose our ability to know them.

Autumn Day reminds me of all of these truths.

It particularly resonates with me this year because, as of late, I've been working hard on clearing my mind in order to be more fully present in my life. I've read three books in ten days that all point to the same challenge: be conscious, be clear, be present. In addition, I have made four agreements with myself (based on the book of the same name, Four Agreements by Don Miguel Ruiz):

"Be impeccable with your word,"

"Don't personalize anything."

"Don't make assumptions."

"Do (my) best."

Easier said than done, especially given my propensity to overthink in the name of keeping everything lined up in their rows, all according to plan.

In faith, I've set these agreements as my new personal mission and have embarked upon it accordingly. Today being Autumn Day, it seems fitting to be on this path of washing out the old and ushering in the new.

Soon after, Mario's paws thumped hard on the bed and he set his big head right in the crook of my neck. It fit perfectly. His whiskers tickled my cheek and his breathing in my ear made me giggle and the weight of his head filled me with love.

As we embarked on our Autumn Day walk, I was not disappointed. No longer a five-minute walk between my door and the water, Mario and I actually had to get into the car to reach the shoreline. I parked and opened the door to cool, clean air, still a bit heavy with the humidity from the previous evening's rain. I walked down and across the street and heard the water lapping on the rocks with the perfect rhythm only nature can play. Along the dirt path this morning were flowers that seemed to have emerged quite quickly, just as they do every time our warm summer turns into a wet autumn overnight. God seems to open a tiny window between the two seasons, and, with the weather in perfect balance, these gifts grow out of the most unexpected places.

There were two kinds of flowers out on the path: a dark, sad, prickly little thistle with small purple flowers almost hiding within the dense leaves; the others, wildflowers, tall, lanky, bright green bunches of stems capped by perfect little bundles of tiny yellow flowers.

As I looked at these flowers, my friend's question from several days before came back to me: was everything I worked for what I wanted, or just what I felt I should have?

The answer: both.

I wanted to be a flower. With my whole heart and mind I set my intention to become one and, against many odds, just as the flowers on this dirt path, I emerged a victor. The problem is, I wasn't clear what kind of flower I actually intended to be. More to the point, I couldn't hear what my true nature longed for me to remember about myself, nor was I clear the price I was going to have to pay to do so. I had become the sad, shrinking thistle, when really what I wanted to be was the tall-standing wildflower.

My faith has always been strong, even stronger than my determination, but I just never understood how one affected the other before. I wanted the house and the family and the neighborhood, and I got them; but I wanted those things because I didn't have them growing up and I feared my children wouldn't either. I wanted more for them; but in going about the process of achieving more for them, I lost myself.

Intention, I'm learning, is exceptionally powerful. It must be approached with a great deal of understanding and attention and, well, intention. What I really want is not the husband and the house and the neighborhood; what I really want is a sense of stability, security, love, fulfillment, and joy; I want to love and be loved in a way that is unencumbered by self-editing and worry. This, to me, is what it means to truly be happy. Attachment to some generic idea of "happy" does me no good. What I must put my energy behind is an intention for what makes me happy, and then allow it to come in the form it is meant to come.

Learning doesn't always come the way I expect it, but it always comes.

In making my way back home with Mario this morning, I see the sun breaking through the clouds and streaming through the leaves of the nearby trees that are just beginning their turn from green to red. That's the thing about Autumn Day—just when I think the warmth of summer is gone, it breaks through to remind me it is always there to warm me, even if I can't see it. After the haze of summer has been washed away, and the winds of autumn days and the quiet of winter days are through, there are many sunny days yet to come.

Spring, so the parting clouds remind me, is just around the corner.

Reach Tall Toward the Sun

"Our deepest fear is not that we are inadequate. Our deepest fear is that we are powerful beyond measure. It is our light, not our darkness, that most frightens us."

- Marianne Williamson, *A Return to Love: Reflections on the Principles of "A Course in Miracles"*

I sit here in the quiet of my apartment. It's in the middle of downtown, yet you wouldn't know it from the stillness around me. Maybe because it's early on Thanksgiving morning; the streets are quiet, the birds are chirping, and as Mario and I lie in this bed together, Thanksgiving is exactly what comes to mind.

I am alone. What I've found in this aloneness is Grace.

I am thankful for many, many things, chief among them this morning is Grace. I have been given the gift of Grace my whole life, things I considered hardships growing up were extraordinary opportunities that I had to experience in order to get to this very place that now feels so right. Now that I am present and quiet, I can hear and see Grace everywhere. All this time I was working so hard to achieve it and little did I know, it was with me all along.

Part of what Grace has given me is this time alone. Ironic, because I have always been afraid of being alone. I've done many things in my life to avoid being alone, some productive and some destructive, because I thought the chief architect of loneliness was Aloneness. In finally allowing myself to sit with that architect, however, I've found that thought untrue. At least for me, it was actually the anticipation and fear of Aloneness that created my loneliness; as soon as I learned to embrace Aloneness it actually brought me Grace. And Grace has connected me to myself and the people I love more than ever before.

I lived with a sense of abandonment growing up, a byproduct of many things including watching my mother repeatedly abandon herself in favor of what others wanted (or what she thought others wanted) as well as an unreliable and inconsistent relationship with my father. I *never* wanted my children to feel that in our home so the toughest thing for me to learn has been that, in allowing them to live with an unhappy mother, I didn't protect them from a sense of abandonment, I perpetuated it. I may not have physically abandoned them, but I did abandon them in other ways. In hiding from myself, I hid from them. In not caring for myself I did not care for them. In not facing my fears I created new fears for them. Only now that I have moved out of the house am I able to be fully present with them every day. Only now can I say with complete conviction that I am the best and most conscious mother I can be.

Ironically, I was granted the time and space to heal, in part, by my unhealthy ambition to do things "right." I started building a career moments after finishing college, married at 25, bought a starter house at 28, bought a bigger house on a cul-de-sac at 32, all while we both worked full time, each with a side hustle ensuring that we could do all this without debt beyond our mortgage. The fuel for this relentless pursuit of financial security was not passion nor pleasure, but the desire to do life "perfectly."

All of that striving for perfection broke me into pieces, yet, part of that striving is also what allowed me the financial means to leave my home in order to get the space I needed to put myself back together. This space has allowed me to see the possibility of a future that looks different from the past—a future that I hope includes my family intact and, whether or not we are under the same roof, each of us able to reach tall into the light of our potential while being anchored by the integrity of our individual truths.

Truth, not perfection.

What is, not what should be.

Dreams of Perfection, I appreciate you. I just no longer need you. You were a gift to me, a gift that helped me strive personally and professionally. Now my gift to you is to let you go and, in your place, allow Truth to dwell.

We have a family tradition of spending part of New Year's Eve writing down our wishes for the coming year and sealing them into an envelope. Like every year, my boys asked what my wishes were, promising they'd forget as soon as I told them, because they know telling a wish means it may not come true.

"My wish is to be healthy, and happy, and feel full of the love of my family."

"That's a boring wish," Jackson replied.

"Yeah, Mom. Don't you want to wish for something like a Wii?" Tommy added.

"Well," I started, "I also wrote down that I wished to write a book."

"That's cool, I guess," Jackson said, "But I still think you should have wished for a Wii."

Craig and I shared a shy smile. Even in our pain our boys can always bring us to common ground. He looked away so quickly, though, leaving me wondering if he was hoping I had wished for something different too.

Driving back to my apartment I was not surprised to see how many people were out; what did strike me, however, was that of all those I saw, no one walked alone. Not only that, no one walked in groups either, only as a part of a pair. Has it always been like this and I've just never noticed? Not having spent a New Year's Eve without someone to kiss at midnight since I was thirteen, I'm not sure I'd ever have reason to notice. All of these years I had someone to kiss at midnight. Tonight there's no one.

If this were last New Year's Eve, I'd be so sad. *Years of kissing on this crazy night and now NO ONE? How can that be? I don't do alone.* By default, I would be frantically searching to fill that void, looking for something, anything, that might be my missing piece.

But this is not last New Year's Eve. I don't need that script anymore.

Nothing's Missing. That's the lesson I'm finally starting to learn.

I know this journey's purpose is, above all, to show me that nothing is missing. Shoving someone or something into what feels like an empty space does little more than block my ability to speak and think and breathe. I have my own career, my own car, make my own money, cook my own food, clean my own house, advocate for my own health and well-being; I make my own choices my own way. I don't need to sacrifice or dance or play any kind of anything to keep that empty spot filled.

In the weeks leading up to the holidays most of my conversations with loved ones included their furrowed brow, their look of concern, their hand on my shoulder as they inquired how I was feeling.

"Have you thought about the holidays? Things should be getting pretty hard soon."

nothing's missing

Maybe they should be, but they're not.
I'm ringing in the new year alone.
And nothing's missing.

I remember a time when I thought loving someone else was all I needed to be happy. Then I realized I also needed that person to love me. Then I realized even though we loved each other, it still wouldn't be enough. I had to find love in my own heart and be ruthless in my quest to heal.

Here I am on the other side of hurt and the way I got here was making the decision to walk through it.

On this other side, I have to find a way to extend the love I've given myself back to Craig. We've made real progress in counseling these past few months and never once did he give up. I was relentlessly selfish at times, not maliciously so but certainly in the name of self-preservation. Craig could have thrown up his hands at any time and called it done, but he didn't. Consciously or not, maybe he knew that I had held on for him all these years and this was his turn to do the same; consciously or not, maybe he knew he had a significant role in why I had spun out so far and so he's been waiting to see if I could find my way back. I'm not sure; I'm also not sure it matters.

What does matter is that, if we come back together, we both have to be very clear about what we want and how we want it. We fell in love and into marriage totally unconsciously; we now have to walk consciously, eyes, minds, and hearts wide open, into a new kind of love and partnership.

my list of what I must have in the giv-
love, because, for me, a good list clarifies

What I Need in Love

- <u>Home</u>. A sweet, cozy home where I feel comfortable, at peace, and loved. My children feel the same. A place I can walk into and intrinsically know that this, in fact, is my home.

- <u>Trust</u>. I want full and total trust that I am safe in my own presence, my own skin, and my own heart. I won't have to look over my shoulder. I don't have to second-guess or wonder or worry because I know this love is my soft place to land. It's a place I feel understood, safe, seen, heard, and adored.

- <u>Teamwork</u>. I want to be a part of a partnership moving toward common goals. I want the goals to be flexible, attainable, and positive and be grounded to a love that is tender, passionate, and joyful. I don't want to compete; I don't want to defend. I want to be "in it together," in action and in spirit.

- <u>Caretaking</u>. I want to take care of someone, and I want that someone to take care of me. I want to give and receive small tokens of kindness multiple times a day, having a meal together and clearing plates, making coffee for the other, saving the favorite section of the paper for the other, bringing home a book the other may like, cleaning the other's car as a small surprise—small acts done with great love.

- Consciousness. I want to have love at the center of the relationship and the center of the home. I want it to be attended to with intention. I want it to be cherished and appreciated, and I want to move forward in a relationship with an awareness of where we are together and how we can continue to support that togetherness as well as our individuality.

- My Own Self. I need time every day to nurture my own self to write, to walk, to be quiet in the daily chores of the house and garden. I want to spend time with friends, attend to loved ones, do something for the community, develop my work and my health and be connected to my own heart as much as I am connected to the hearts of those I love.

- A Family. More than perhaps any of the other things, I want a family. A full, noisy house of kids and animals—a joyous madness that is embraced with gratitude and laughter and the knowing that all souls moving in and out are welcomed there, are cherished there, that they can fight and wrestle, can hug and snuggle, and can feel that in this moment and in this family they are loved above all else.

I don't know if I can achieve this under the current structure that exists. What I do know, however, is that this is the kind of love I want and will accept no other.

115

My sleeping place is in an old, drafty building. Downright cold in February, I had to invite my dog into bed to prevent both of us from shivering. Now spring, I'm surprised to find I feel not much warmer. It feels colder. Much colder. Drafty isn't the half of it—it's more like, windy.

Why? There's a huge hole in my roof.

It rained here the last couple days, a kind of crazy rain that doesn't usually happen in the spring. It's an old building, but from what I understand a fairly new roof. I suppose a roof, much like a person, can only take so much until it comes crashing down.

I know something about this. Apparently, so does my roof.

Why is it that, with three units on the top floor, only the portion of the roof over my kitchen gave way to the rains? It must have been collecting water for months until one day it burst open and a very dramatic crashing down of water resulted.

Had I been living at home, this would have been my husband's issue to deal with. I would take care of the kids and the pets and the belongings and he would be on the phone dealing with the problem that created the mess I was cleaning up. Here, though, it's all me.

Friday nights are sleepover nights; I pick up the kids from school, head downtown for some hang out time at the library, dinner out, and then we huddle up at the "sleeping place" with the dog on the large chair I generously call a couch to watch a video. This Friday night, however, the library books and the kids and the dog had to be ushered home—quickly—as I dealt with the property management on the phone.

Save my favorite calendar and some old notebooks on the floor, everything dried out soon after the hole was patched and the water was removed. A (very minor) natural would-be disaster occurred and, look at me, I did just fine.

This is not the *Fine* so often paired with Should. This is the fine my ninth grade English teacher, an elderly lady who still used the word gay to describe someone who was joyful and didn't understand why the class giggled every time. When she used fine she meant it as the ultimate compliment. In fact, I decided I was going to teach students how to write the day I got the reflective essay I wrote about my dad's third divorce and the impact it had on my ability to trust myself back with her scrawly handwriting across the top, underlined for emphasis, "FINE!"

I wasn't fine because I should be. I was fine because I felt FINE! I had to spend some time away from the sleeping place, at home with my family for the two days it took for repairs and clean up. Another would-be disaster six months ago, now feels like a blessing. I was home for two days and, look at me, I did FINE!

I know an ode is some kind of tribute; beyond that, I'm not so sure. Is it like a sonnet with a prescribed style or iambic pentameter? I'm not sure about that either. I should probably look that up, but I'm okay not knowing. I just want to give my sleeping place its due honor; an "ode" feels like just the thing.

I sit at this little table by the drafty window in my tiny apartment like I do every Sunday. Only this time, instead of being surrounded by beautiful things and pictures and feeling enveloped by the love I created here, there are only hooks left on the picture rail and Mario's nails clicking on the bare wood floor and echoing off the empty walls as he looks for a place to cozy up. Cozy. That was this apartment. I created a cozy, warm, affectionate space just for us.

Sleeping Place, I'm leaving you, jumping into a faith that you helped me create, a faith that is taking me back home.

Home. I slept at home last night and I woke up this morning to my family, a bunch of boys—gassy, giggling, noisy boys—and all the critical elements of a morning with small children in the house: TV, cereal, getting up as soon as humanly possible for both.

A joyous madness. I've missed it.

When I am done packing up this apartment today, I will go home for good, as long as "good" is meant to be. Can I create the kind of cozy, warm, affectionate space at home that I had here in my sleeping place? Here was just for me and my dog. We cried here. We laughed here. We healed here, he and I. The joyous madness of home fills my heart; this apartment, it filled my soul. I have to find a way to bring both together in the peace of what I want my life to be.

So, Sleeping Place, I leave you today. You came to me at the perfect time. Everyone told me not to leave my house and come to you, but you spoke to me and I knew here is where I was meant to be. You showed me a whole new way of living. You helped me face my fear of being alone. Actually, with you I never felt alone. Between you and Mario, I felt sandwiched by what I've come to know as Grace.

Sitting empty, you are no longer the apartment I knew. You are preparing yourself for someone else. I watch Mario now chasing his tail and tossing his toy into his food bowl, and I see a freedom in him I haven't seen here in your place. When we moved here, he knew our purpose was quiet healing; now he knows it's time to set off on the next leg of our journey toward freedom, freedom from the heartache that the two of you helped me release.

You took my hurt into your walls. Come to think of it, maybe that explains the flood in the kitchen a few weeks ago. You were the only one in our whole building that was impacted by that storm— why is that? Did my heartache blow a hole through the roof? And when you let in all that water and I had to sleep at my house for two nights, were you telling me the time had come to go home?

It seems the time has come for me to go home.

I'm free, aren't I? I'm almost overwhelmed at the prospect. I'm a little afraid of it, but not the paralyzing fear that used to plague me.

It's more a humbling anticipation; the kind of that knows I'm in exactly the right place to finally fly. I'm hesitant to leave my nest; I love it here and it scares me to let it go. And I also know flying is what this nest has prepared me to do.

"Fly Free," you say.

And Free, I am.

Everyday Grace

"I do not at all understand the mystery
of grace –

Only that it meets us where we are but does not
leave us where it found us."

-Anne Lamott, *Traveling Mercies: Some Thoughts
on Faith*

For most of my life up until this point, my heart, body, and mind busied me with worry so I didn't have to deal with my fear. After many years of unrecognized and unnamed struggle, I heard its call and walked toward it.

Now my fear, for the most part, is gone. I'm okay alone just as I'm ok married. I'm okay healthy just as I would be okay battling a disease. I can even say that, at least in theory, I'm okay with healthy children just as I would be okay —eventually—if something were to happen to them. The point is, no matter what, I'm okay.

And that's what all people grounded in the truth have in common: no matter where they are, they're okay.

And I am okay.

I still hear myself asking, "Who do you think you are?" when I attempt to reach tall toward the sun. I finished 85% of this book, for example, in 2010; it's being published in 2022. What pushed me to finally get over myself, to finally make this particularly public and vulnerable reach, was twofold: my desire to honor my aging dog and the role he played in my healing and my even deeper desire for women around this country, especially in the aftermath of a global pandemic, to be strong and brave and vulnerable enough to stand on their tip-toes as they reach as high as they can, turning their uniquely important light up as bright as they can. Our collective light has never been more powerful, and it has never been more important.

What would our grandmothers and great grandmothers say to us if we told them we didn't want to be too brave? Or too educated? Or too pretty? Or too successful? The practical, reserved, non-Italian ones in my family would shake their heads at me in confusion, maybe offer a "You know better than that" phrase of some kind; the Italian women would not be so understated.

At me they'd likely shout, "How could you do this to us?" Code among Italians for a lot of things, in this case it would mean, "We did all this for you; we sacrificed all this for you; how dare you disrespect our work by not maximizing every opportunity you have?" Some may call that a guilt trip—we call it dinner conversation.

Either way, I know turning my light up is the best thing I can do to magnify the lights of my grandmothers. In response, and thanks to my translate app, which may or may not be getting this right, I can almost hear them say, "*Siame cosi orgogliose di te.*"

We're so proud of you.

And I'd say, "*Grazie, per sempre.*"

Thank you, forever.

Nicole Lusiani

ACKNOWLEDGEMENTS

During what was the most difficult time of my life and marriage, when I was living alone in a tiny, cold apartment in the middle of winter, Craig forwarded me an email about a writing workshop led by the most amazing Mary Thompson Reynolds. We were in a precarious financial position and a dire emotional place, but he remembered my New Year's wish; and how he responded to my hesitancy about the writing workshop changed my life.

"If you want to do it, don't let anything stop you," he said. "Not your fear, not the cost, and certainly not me." Mary, I wrote the damned book, and I am deeply grateful for your encouragement and support.

To the earliest and most recent readers of this book, 2010 and 2019 respectively, Tovi and Pam. How I got so lucky to land you as my soul sister and soul mama I will never know. And to all the readers in between: Evangeline, Alison, Valerie, Lydia, Mary, Tina, Keith, and Craig, look what we built together. Thank you for your honesty, your love, and your ass-kicking support.

I was struck by divine inspiration one day when, on a whim, I googled, "Who is Jen Hatmaker's publicist?" I knew I had a pretty good book on my hands and I also knew I had big intentions for its service in the world and I couldn't do that alone. Jen had always talked on her socials so lovingly about her team, something in me thought, Why not me? This inspired question brought me to the incomparable Heather Adams and her team at Choice Communications. From there I was delivered to the team at Yates and Yates. These two companies and the incredible humans who created them taught me, nudged me, and inspired in me the courage and know how to get this book into your hands. For them, and for you, I'm so grateful.

To my family and friends who created the safety net under my tight rope so I could thrive as a woman, wife, mother, teacher, and writer, I thank you. I am blessed beyond measure to inhabit your village.

I speak often in this book of the women in my life who helped me become who I am. I know that, not only do I not do their contributions justice, I also do not mention all of them. Some are fresher in my mind, some are more present in my life; all of them, however, are important. To all those who came before me, my great grandmothers, grandmothers, aunts, and cousins, as well as those who served as extended mothers, aunts, and cousins, I offer my thanks and love.

And to those who are coming after, particularly the students in my Women's Studies classes from 2002-2013, what a gift you were to me. You did every crazy thing I asked you to do, read, watch, discuss (and draw!). In doing so, you taught me more about what it meant to be a woman than anyone ever had before. You were vulnerable, vulnerable enough to share your wounds so we knew we were not alone and vulnerable enough to share your laughter so we knew there was always hope. I carry that infinite hope forward knowing that you are now adults and the leaders we have all been waiting for. Thank you for being my teachers, each and every one of you. And thank you to my friend, colleague, and fellow Mama, Dana, who opened the possibility of teaching this extraordinary class. It changed not only the lives of our kids, it also changed mine.

Although I fear making myself a cliché, I would be remiss not to mention Oprah Winfrey by name given she was the person who met me every day after school from my freshman year in high school in 1986 to the end of my 16th year as a high school teacher, when her show went off the air in 2011. She and the guests she featured on her show changed the trajectory of my life, so much so that her life's work is imprinted on my soul. To her and all the people who made her show possible, I offer my profound thanks.

To my mom, who taught me to throw my seeds far and wide even when she couldn't herself. We all stand on the shoulders of those who walked before us; perhaps no greater example exists than me standing on yours.

To my sons, the boys I was born to nurture and empower and love. There will never be words to adequately express just how much I love you. I wrote this book for you in hopes you will see that falling is just as valuable as getting back up. Dad and I didn't stay together for you, but we surely worked harder because of you—one of the many ways you both inspire me every day to be a stronger, better human being. I was never more blessed than the days you each arrived in my body and in my heart.

To Craig, my greatest teacher and my greatest love. You have pushed me through doors I was afraid to open and held me up to the light when I wanted to hide. The tapestry of our life together is one for which I would not trade a thread, especially the threads that had to be ripped apart and then mended in order to be appreciated in full.

And to my dog, whose unconditional love and incessant need to be walked brought me back to myself, even when I didn't know I'd gone missing. The ten years you were on the scene would have looked so much different without you. Quite simply, you taught me God is love, and so is Dog.

Thank you.

A BIBLIOGRAPHY, OF SORTS

Much of this story was written as an act of personal cathar-sis—a journal of sorts dedicated to processing the over-whelming questions for which I had neither context nor answers. It must be said that, in addition to the journaling, the reading and listening I did over the course of this year had a hugely positive impact on my emotional well-being. While I couldn't possibly reference all the conversations, stories, and songs that liberated me during this time, I can acknowledge the gifts given to me by the writers of the books I read, people who filled my life with hope in what felt like a very hopeless time.

On this journey I read some of these books for the first time; alternatively, the opportunity to reread others brought me a whole new level of understanding. Recently my therapist said, "I'm not sure you need me anymore, right now anyway." If she was right, it's at least in part due to the wisdom of these gifted authors who were willing to vulnerably speak their truth.

To each of you, my heartfelt thanks. You liberated me to brave-ly stand in my truth, just as audaciously as you had to do in order to write these books. In doing so, you allowed me to write one of my own.

In alphabetical order, I thank the following

- Alvarez, Julia. (1994) *In the Time of Butterflies*
- Angelou, Maya. (1993). *Wouldn't Take Nothing for my Journey Now*
- Beck, Martha. (2008). *Steering By Starlight: Find your right life, no matter what*
- Cisneros, Sandra. (1984). *The House on Mango Street*
- Coelho, Paulo. (1993). *The Alchemist* (Alan R. Clarke, Trans.)
- Gilbert, Elizabeth. (2006). *Eat, Pray, Love: One woman's search for everything across Italy, India and Indonesia*
- Grogan, John. (2005). *Marley and Me: Life and love with the world's worst dog*
- Kidd, Sue Monk. (2003) *The Secret Lives of Bees*
- Lamott, Anne. (1999). *Traveling Mercies: Some thoughts on faith*
- Lesser, Elizabeth. (2005). *Broken Open: How difficult times can help us grow*
- Lewis, C.S. (1960). *The Four Loves*
- Morrison, Toni (1970). *The Bluest Eye*
- Morrison, Toni. (1973). *Sula*
- McCarthy, Auriela. (2008). *The Power of the Possible*
- Ruiz, Don Miguel. (1997) *Four Agreements*

- Spragins, Ellyn (Ed). (2006) *What I Know Now, Lessons to My Younger Self*
- Tolle, Eckhart. (2005). *A New Earth: Awakening your life's purpose*
- Vanzant, Iyanla. (1998). *In the Meantime: Finding yourself and the love you want*
- Virtue, Doreen. (2008). *The Miracles of Archangel Michael*
- Williamson, Marianne. (1992). *A Return to Love: Reflections on the principles in the* "Course of Miracles"
- Young, William P. (2007). *The Shack*
- Zukav, Gary. (1989). *The Seat of the Soul*

IN MEMORY OF

mario Lugiani
Elliott

2006*(ish)*-2020

ABOUT THE AUTHOR

Nicole Lusiani is a writer, educator, podcaster, and mother. At the center of all these endeavors is a true knowing that there is no such thing as other people's children because we belong to one another.

The work of Nicole's heart is writing. In 2010 her blog was her first foray into writing publicly, followed soon after by *Skills I Wish I Learned in School: Building a Research Paper* and *The Wildflower Manifesto*. She's the host of the weekly podcast, *Copy Room Conversations*, serving teachers in a way she hopes will fuel them and remind them just how important their work is. This is her first memoir.

Nicole's day job includes work for the Center to Support Excellence in Teaching (CSET) at Stanford University and the Center for Culturally Responsive Teaching and Learning, where she focuses her professional development and instructional coaching on instructional equity. Prior to this, Nicole served as a public high school teacher for twenty years.

Nicole's favorite thing to do is hang out with her teenage children and the family dog, the group of whom make up her strongest circle of love and Joyous Madness.

***

Learn more at Nicole's work at NicoleLusiani.com

CPSIA information can be obtained
at www.ICGtesting.com
Printed in the USA
LVHW111634070622
720696LV00004B/329

9 780990 522393